CAMBRIDGE IBERIAN AND
LATIN AMERICAN STUDIES

GENERAL EDITOR
PROFESSOR P. E. RUSSELL, F.B.A.
PROFESSOR OF SPANISH STUDIES, THE UNIVERSITY OF OXFORD

Galdós and the irony of language

Galdós and the irony of language

DIANE F. UREY

ILLINOIS STATE UNIVERSITY

CAMBRIDGE UNIVERSITY PRESS

CAMBRIDGE

LONDON   NEW YORK   NEW ROCHELLE

MELBOURNE   SYDNEY

For Mark

Published by the Press Syndicate of the University of Cambridge
The Pitt Building, Trumpington Street, Cambridge CB2 1RP
32 East 57th Street, New York, NY 10022, USA
296 Beaconsfield Parade, Middle Park, Melbourne 3206, Australia

© Cambridge University Press 1982

First published 1982

Printed in Great Britain by
Western Printing Services Ltd, Bristol

Library of Congress catalog card number: 81–12210

British Library Cataloguing in Publication Data
Urey, Diane F.
Galdós and the irony of language.
(Cambridge Iberian and Latin American studies)
1. Pérez Galdós, Benito
I. Title
863'.5   PQ6555.25
ISBN 0 521 23756 4

Contents

Acknowledgements   vi

Introduction   1

1   The irony of portrait   5
    Isidora Rufete
    Rosalía de Bringas

2   The setting of irony   47
    La de Bringas
    Torquemada y San Pedro
    Nazarín
    Misericordia

3   The narrator of irony   64
    The historical chronicle, the novel within the novel, and
    Don Quijote: *Nazarín* and *Halma*
    'Phantom chapters': *Ángel Guerra*
    First-person narrators: *El amigo Manso* and *Lo prohibido*
    The epistolary novel: *La incógnita*
    The dialogue novel: *Realidad*

4   The texture of irony   95

Conclusion   122

Notes   129

Bibliography   134

Index   137

Acknowledgements

This book had its genesis as a doctoral dissertation at The Johns Hopkins University under the direction of Professor Paul R. Olson. I owe an enormous debt to Professor Olson for the careful and enthusiastic guidance which he offered at every stage of my graduate studies. I am also deeply grateful for the advice provided by Professor Harry Sieber, the second reader of my dissertation at Johns Hopkins, and for the inspiration of Professor Robert M. Jackson, who first introduced me to Galdós while I was an undergraduate at the University of Oregon. Lastly, I want to thank my husband, Mark Johnston, who took many hours from his own research in Spanish literature to help me with the painstaking revision and correction of the typescript.

Introduction

The novels of Benito Pérez Galdós reflect the influence of Cervantes, eighteenth- and nineteenth-century English authors, the French Romantics, Balzac, Flaubert, Zola, Dostoevsky, Tolstoy, and many others. Galdós refined the narrative techniques he learned from their novels, and in some respects his original adaptations of the genre were more advanced than those of any other contemporary European author. Galdós' knowledge of Cervantes fostered his own acute use of irony, to which the so-called realist mode of narrative seems naturally inclined. 'Irony', Northrop Frye has declared, 'as a mode, is born from the low mimetic; it takes life exactly as it finds it.'[1] Sophisticated irony, in its claim to objectivity, refuses to judge life and thus forces the reader to define it for himself.

Although the sense of the term irony may seem intuitively obvious, no single definition will exhaustively comprehend it. Traditionally, it refers to the figure of speech which involves 'saying one thing and meaning another'.[2] In literary theory of the twentieth century it has come to be used in a much broader sense, to refer to the concept of a relation of disparity or inadequacy. It is in this structural and relational sense that the term is used in the critical theory of Gÿorgy Lukács, Northrop Frye, Wayne Booth, and numerous others.[3] An ironical situation is that which exists between an observer and an observed who is not aware of being observed. The narrative situation of the reader and that which he reads, for example, can therefore be seen as intrinsically ironic. Scholes and Kellogg have written in *The Nature of Narrative* that 'The narrative situation is thus ineluctably ironical. The quality of irony is built into the narrative form as it is into no other form of literature.'[4] Since the observer feels superior to that which he is observing, he feels pleasure. 'Our pleasure in narrative literature itself, then, can be seen as a function of disparity of viewpoint [between ourselves and the characters, for example] or irony' (Scholes and Kellogg, p. 241).

Besides the implicit irony of the narrative relationship between text and reader, there is an irony which is constantly made explicit in the novels of Pérez Galdós. This explicit irony produces various effects; chiefly it unmasks superficiality by revealing a conflicting interiority which contradicts it. Such an irony can serve many purposes and can be found everywhere. D. C. Muecke begins his study, *The Compass of Irony*, with the following observations:

Irony may be a weapon in a satirical attack, or a smokescreen concealing a retreat, or a device for turning the world or oneself inside out; irony may be found in words and attitudes, in events and situations; or we may find nothing on earth and quite certainly nothing in heaven that is not ironic.[5]

Such strategies of irony pervade Galdós' novels, educating the reader not to be too self-assured, not to believe everything he reads, and not to give too much credence to his own powers of objectivity.

Galdós manipulates the pretense of objectivity in his novels in order to ask if there is indeed any objective view at all. This manipulation is displayed in numerous quixotic characters whose subjective views prohibit them from seeing clearly and in the presentation of the entire narration itself as fiction. The language of Galdós' novels reveals the irony of language itself. Their representational models are applicable not only to the social world, but to all concepts of representation, which are constantly undermined. The claim of objectivity and realism in Galdós' novels is an attempt to depict accurately not only the customs of society, but the conventions of perception which function in that society. Robert Alter, in 'History and Imagination in the 19th Century Novel', writes:

There is, however, another direction taken by the realist impulse in the novel, in which the primary object of critical and imaginative attention is not the social world and the historical moment as they bear down on individual lives, but rather, the instruments of fictional representation themselves. This self-conscious tradition – in which the novel is devised to flaunt systematically its own condition as artifice in order to test the problematic relationship between fiction and reality – begins with the very beginning of the genre in *Don Quixote*.[6]

The novel as a construct of language can never escape the question of what language is within the context of a subjectively comprehended reality which is itself illusory.

This study examines the narrative devices which lead the reader of Galdós to perceive the irony of the novel – whether in a character, in a situation, or in the contradiction which is intrinsic to the realist claim of objective representation. Galdós' novels continually subvert those conventions of reading with which the reader seeks to make the novel intelligible, especially those by which he postulates the correspondence of its representations to his own social, cultural, and literary milieu. Irony extends the reader's constant drive to 'seek the truth', to 'solve the enigma'. Irony dramatizes the choice the reader must make among several alternative appearances of 'truth' in the novel, and it thus makes him a more active participant in the production of meaning in the text.

Since the reader himself forms a 'text' of his own knowledge and experience, he is, like the novel, also a construct of 'intertextualities' or 'intersubjectivities'. Jonathan Culler, in *Structuralist Poetics*, describes the conventions of reading by which the reader attempts to relate his texts of acquired knowledge to that of the novel. He calls this process 'naturalization', because the reader continually attempts to make the literary text 'vraisemblable'.

The *vraisemblable* is thus the basis of the important structuralist concept of *intertextualité*: the relation of a particular text to other texts...A work can only be read in connection with or against other texts, which provide a grid through which it is read and structured by establishing expectations which enable one to pick out salient features and give them a structure. And hence intersubjectivity – the shared knowledge which is applied in reading – is a function of these other texts.[7]

When this knowledge which is shared between a literary text and the text of a reader is manipulated or reversed, then irony – including that of the reader himself – is effected. Wayne Booth describes in *A Rhetoric of Irony* (p. 33) the process of perceiving or 'reconstructing' irony. 'Ironic reconstructions', he writes, 'depend on an appeal to assumptions, often unstated, that ironists and readers share.' These assumptions are often subtly subverted in Galdós' works to create complex ironies in the relation between the novel and the reader. Irony is both a mode of novelistic control and a way of viewing the world. Galdós' novels ironize the reader who is inattentive or narrow-minded, just as they ironize the pretended status of their own discourse as an approximation of 'life'. Lukács saw such irony in any attempt to create a homogeneous idea – like the presumed representational or 'meaning-ful' novel – from a heterogeneous world. The moment the idea is formed, negating discrete 'reality', it is paradoxically abolished by that same reality. 'This interaction of two ethical complexes, their duality as to form and their unity in being given form, is the content of irony, which is the normative mentality of the novel' (p. 84). More recently Culler has observed: 'The novel is an ironic form born of the discrepancy between meaning and experience, whose source of value lies in the interest of exploring that gap and filling it, while knowing that any claim to have filled it derives from blindness.'[8] This global novelistic irony is implicit in any novel at all levels. It is epitomized in the hero who is destroyed when he attempts to realize his ideas. It is also the irony of the writer – and the reader – who assumes that he can apprehend, describe, or interpret anything with complete objectivity. And it is the irony of reality itself in that it can never completely subsume ideals, but continually gives rise to the ideals which are manifested in language. Irony reveals the pretense of the assumption that meaning can be defined or delimited.

Muecke has described three principal ways of employing irony:

Irony may be used as a rhetorical device to enforce one's meaning. It may be used...as a satiric device to attack a point of view or to expose folly, hypocrisy, or vanity. It may be used as an heuristic device to lead one's readers to see that things are not so simple or certain as they seem, or perhaps not so complex or doubtful as they seem. (Muecke, pp. 232–3)

In Galdós' works all three of these methods, and variations of them, are present. This study attempts to analyze these methods as they work in concert and individually. It is divided into four chapters, 'The irony of portrait', 'The setting of irony', 'The narrator of irony', and 'The texture of irony'. In this last chapter the observations made in the first three chapters will be consolidated and applied to one novella, *Torquemada en la hoguera*.

This analysis does not pretend to be either an exhaustive or a chronological reading of Galdós' work. What it seeks to offer is an illustration of the range of sophistication and development in his literary creation and to prepare the way for future studies of this type. Thematic, stylistic, and interpretive functions will all be considered; they are invoked separately and in connection with each other according to their contribution to the ironic effect. Selected novels from Galdós' *serie contemporánea*, his most acclaimed works, will be studied in the hope that the passages chosen will prove to be representative, not merely because they are taken from those novels which are most obviously ironic, but because they demonstrate how irony is latent throughout Galdós' work, as it is in language itself.

I

The irony of portrait

Character is no less an artificial construct than are the other elements of the novel. But the seemingly natural device of the proper name effects the conventional emergence of the literary construct which is the character's 'personality'. Through the postulation that he conforms to a model (both literary and cultural), a character has meaning particularly for the reader of the nineteenth-century novel. The artifice which creates this illusion can be analyzed at many levels. Roland Barthes illustrates how 'when identical semes traverse the same proper name several times and appear to settle upon it, a character is created'.[1] In Galdós' ironic art the various 'semes', or connotations, which traverse the character often derive from contradictory or incompatible literary, cultural, or social 'codes', and thus their concurrence forms an ironic portrait. In many of his novels, the protagonist is the axis around which these literary, cultural, and social codes revolve. The irony of the portrait, therefore, reveals and is reflected in that of the other units of meaning that converge upon and re-emerge from the locus of the character, weaving the total text. The two figures studied in this chapter, Isidora Rufete and Rosalía de Bringas, are both 'characters' whose 'personalities' and 'attitudes' form the ironic nexus of their novels.

La desheredada (1881) was the first of Galdós' *Novelas contemporáneas* and as such marks an important turning point in his artistic style. For with this novel he leaves behind the strong tendency to polemics and the rather stereotyped characters to which this gives rise. Isidora Rufete is a large and dominating figure whose illusions are revealed with great creativity. With this novel Galdós employs various narrative modes, not all of them found before in his work. The result is a penetrating study of the human conflict that exists between 'illusion' and 'reality'.

Tormento and *La de Bringas* (both published in 1884) form a double

5

portrait of Rosalía de Bringas that further elaborates certain thematic and structural elements already developed in the portrait of Isidora. The two characters can be aptly compared in order to demonstrate the variations in Galdós' ironic strategies. *La de Bringas* displays subtle refinements on some of the narrative devices seen in *La desheredada* and generally offers a more tightly woven ironic construct. Moreover, Rosalía's process of learning to live with the reality of society's fiction is an ironic statement on Isidora who never reconciles her fiction with social realities. Both reveal the dilemma of the reader who must make the transition from observer to observed and back again. In other words, these portraits display at many levels the problems of objectively viewing the phenomenon of 'character', both in others – including literary personalities – and in the reader's self.

If the narrative situation is intrinsically ironic in positing the duality of the observer and the observed – or the reader and the readable – *La desheredada* multiplies the irony implicit in narrative itself. Like *Don Quijote*, which it both parallels and parodies, *La desheredada* relates both the adventures of a misreader of fiction and fiction's own distance from reality.[2] The reader can fall victim to this novel's irony if he, like Isidora, fails to heed the textual clues to her 'reality' and reads her as he would any other heroine of a *folletín*.[3] Just as Isidora loses her identity when she finally realizes that she is not the disinherited granddaughter of a *marquesa*, so the reader will be violently displaced in his role if he has not re-evaluated his relation to the values and ideas which she seems to represent. This proviso applies especially to the uncritical reader who sees through Isidora's eyes and ignores the ironic 'superiority' provided by the narrator's vision. Like the barely educated, poverty-stricken orphan girl from Tomelloso (near El Toboso) who identifies herself with the novels she reads, the naive reader may sympathize too long with Isidora's desires.

Yet even for the most careful reader, the suggestions of Isidora's reprehensible nature in her portrait are often ambiguous: the narration invites the reader to pity as well as to condemn her, and she is a victim, albeit a vain one. The function of Isidora's claim to the *marquesado* is more than the catalyst to her actions and the dénouement of the story. It is not until the end of Part I that the reader can be sure her goal is illusory. Expectations are constantly revived and never totally thwarted. The reader is continually forced to re-evaluate the meager details he receives about the protagonist's background. This play between anticipation and partial disclosure compels involvement, as Iser has pointed out in *The Implied Reader*, and this active reader may well fall victim to the text's irony.[4] Such a risk enhances the lesson which *La desheredada* offers in reading narrative and in reading the fictions of society which it examines.

The double-edged irony of Isidora Rufete is sharpened by her representative status, which is emphasized even before the heroine herself appears. Isidora seems to portray a large part of Spain that suffers from an inferior social and moral education. The reader must recognize that Isidora has a distorted, highly subjective view of herself and of the surrounding world. The opening scene in Madrid's asylum for the insane, Leganés, outlines the prevalence of this essential ironic conflict between appearance and reality, and extends it with vivid imagery to the Madrid of the reader which lies beyond the asylum's walls. The dangers inherent in the overzealous pursuit of an idealized illusion (however shallow it might be) must be brought home to the reader. The uncertain region that separates sanity from madness is nowhere more apparent than in the first scenes and characters encountered. The opening statement is a frenzied monologue by Isidora's father, Tomás Rufete, a patient in Leganés. His fantasies, it will eventually be revealed, inspired Isidora's pursuit of her illusive identity. The narrator's comment about this madman is similar to those he makes later about Isidora herself: '¿Hállase en el punto central de la vida, o en miserable decrepitud? La movilidad de sus facciones y el llamear de sus ojos, ¿anuncian exaltado ingenio, o desconsoladora imbecilidad? No es fácil decirlo, ni el espectador, oyéndole y viéndole, sabe decidirse entre la compasión y la risa.'[5] The narrator questions his audience and feigns ignorance, distancing himself from the character and encouraging us to move closer. Both Isidora and Tomás Rufete, who prefigures her, are comical and pitiable figures. The ambivalence of this need both to ridicule and to pity leaves judgment to the reader. This makes the decision more actively the reader's own, as Booth and Iser have shown.[6] Because doubt about Rufete's sanity will play a crucial role in evaluating Isidora's quest for nobility, the reader's judgment is particularly important here. Like Don Quijote, Tomás Rufete becomes lucid before he dies, recognizing that he is in Leganés. Yet in the same breath, his last, he mentions his children and the Marquesa. The reader is left to ponder the truth of the dying man's words, and thus Isidora's identity.

The narrator's explicit call for us to judge a situation is only one of the various devices used to promote participation within the text. The free indirect style, which fuses the voice of the narrator with that of the character, requires the reader to decide who is speaking and to evaluate those words.[7] Demonstrative pronouns followed by a relative clause ('she was one of those who...') invoke a cultural comparison with which the reader is assumed to be familiar, and extend the same familiarity to the fictional object. Another device, which includes the reader more directly, is the use of the first person plural. After describing the horrors of the male ward at Leganés, the precarious balance between the 'sane' reader and the madman is made explicit:

¡Y considerar que aquella triste colonia no representa otra cosa que la exageración o el extremo irritativo de nuestras múltiples particularidades morales o intelectuales!...Porque no, no son tan grandes las diferencias. Las ideas de estos desgraciados son nuestras ideas, pero desengarzadas, sueltas, sacadas de la misteriosa hebra que gallardamente las enfila... 'Hay muchos cuerdos que son locos razonables.' Esta sentencia es de Rufete. (IV. 967)

More parallels follow: the patio is like the Bolsa in its exaggerated egoism, the cruel carcelero–enfermeros are like the ever-vigilant State. Rufete is always concerned with his bien parecer, and is compared to an untiring orator who talks even to himself. As in the passage quoted above, the narrative first draws general comparisons which speak to the reader's world and then narrows them to the particular world of the novel, thus establishing a transitive relationship of correspondence between the character and the reader. This process is circular: Rufete's infirmities are just an exaggeration of our own; moreover, they have contributed to Isidora's, which repeat them. In turn, Isidora's plight, her frivolous yearnings to be what she is not, and her lack of restraint in seeking that goal – even to her final social and moral death – differ little, the narrator indicates, from the actions of many who consider themselves sane, including the reader. Although the novel never finally states whether Isidora is truly mad, the ironic foreshadowing of this first chapter admits her proximity to insanity.[8] In a brief description of the female section of Leganés the narrator's refusal to judge is again evident: 'las hijas de Eva inspiran sentimientos de difícil determinación' (IV. 969). The passage ends significantly with 'Hay una que corre por pasillos y salas buscando su propia persona' (IV. 970). This statement is almost immediately followed by the introduction of Isidora, who later searches the 'pasillos' and 'salas' of the Marquesa's palace for her 'propia persona'.

Isidora's entrance into the narrative initially evokes sympathy from the reader because her first words appear in the free indirect style: 'Quería ver al señor director, al señor facultativo, quería ver a un enfermo, a su señor padre...quería ver el establecimiento; quería entregar una cosa...quería decir otra cosa' (IV. 970). The free indirect style occurs in *La desheredada* and much of Galdós' other work 'for the frequent evocations of inward struggle and spiritual search that attend most moments of tension' (Pascal, p. 81). The impression of confusion and turbulence is restated in the narrator's own words: 'Estos múltiples deseos, que se encerraban en uno solo, fueron expresados atropelladamente y con turbación por la muchacha.' The picture of sweet desperation is further enhanced by the contrast between her rude but quaint costume and her beauty. She inspires a compassionate reaction: 'Ello es que su pañuelo rojo, sus lágrimas acabadas de secar, su gabán raído y de muy difícil calificación en indumentaria, su agraciado rostro, su ademán de resignación, sus botas mayores que los pies y ya entradas en días, inspiraban lástima' (IV. 970). This preliminary perspective soon becomes ironic as she begins talking with the director's scribe, Canencia, whom she only later learns is another *loco-cuerdo*. He addresses her as 'señorita' and the narrator explains: 'A Isidora – ¿por qué ocultarlo? – le gustó que le llamaran señorita. Pero como su ánimo no estaba para vanidades, fijó toda su atención en las palabras consoladoras que había oído, contestando a ellas con una mirada y un hondísimo suspiro' (IV. 971). At this point several aspects of Isidora's personality and of the narrative technique of portrayal emerge. She is rather vain and she dissimulates her feelings to fit the situation, detracting from the sincerity of her grief. The phrase, 'Pero como su ánimo no estaba para vanidades, fijó toda su atención' ironically directs attention to her vain reaction while pretending to discount it. The ensuing conversation with Canencia not only confirms in Isidora a pride and certain shallow sincerity which borders on the melodramatic, it also demonstrates her ignorance. Canencia consoles her with elaborate commonplaces to which she responds with an excessive esteem for his gentlemanliness and intelligence; she thinks he is a priest. After more courteous gestures by Canencia, the use of the free indirect style to describe her reaction enables us to view more intimately her subjective consciousness:[9] 'Isidora estaba encantada. La discreta palabra de aquel buen señor, realizada por un metal de voz muy dulce; su urbanidad sin tacha, un no sé qué de tierno, paternal y simpático que en su semblante había, cautivaban a la dolorida joven, inspirándole tanta admiración como gratitud' (IV. 972). The free indirect style begins here with the word 'discreta' since it later becomes obvious that the narrator's designation of Canencia as discrete could only be ironic. However, the passage has an initial appearance of objectivity which supports Isidora's own assessment of the scribe. This is one of the most subtle ironical effects achieved by the free indirect style. As Pascal explains in *The Dual Voice*, the free indirect style is just that: the voice of the narrator and of the character at once: 'free indirect speech is never purely and simply the evocation of a character's thought and perception, but always bears, in its vocabulary, its intonation, its syntactical composition and other stylistic features, in its content, or its context, or in some combination of these, the mark of the narrator' (p. 43). So while the use of the free indirect style can portray sympathy and invoke the reader's familiarity with a character's subjectivity, because it depends upon the narrator's familiarity, it frequently serves to present an ironic view of that subjectivity. As Spitzer observed, the free indirect style is the voice of mimicry – both of the mimicker and the mimicked (Pascal, p. 29). The subtlety of this effect, as in the above example, may lead the reader to join the character in being mimicked if he fails to note the ironic duality of the voice. The passage underscores Isidora's ignorance by demonstrating her inability to judge character and recognize the commonplace. Moreover, her appreciation for Canencia's enchanting, courteous manner overshadows the consoling aim of the words. The placing of 'admiración' before 'gratitud' brings this into relief. All these confidences increase her natural expansive tendencies and reveal what she believes to be her true identity. In doing so, she exposes aspects of her personality of which she is never aware.

Canencia speaks of how all must work together for divine harmony, whatever the cost; yet Isidora's thoughts turn not to the image of divine will, but rather to a selfish contemplation of her own burden: 'Esta sentencia afectó a la de Rufete, haciéndole pensar en lo cara que a ella sola le costaba la armonía de todos. Enjugándose otra vez en las lágrimas, dijo así:...' (IV. 972). Although several aspects of her account of her poverty-stricken childhood provoke compassion, the importance of the subsequent relation is its ironic forecast. A process which is frequently used in the portrayal of Isidora is self-characterization through description of others; in this first instance it is through her assessment of her father that she reveals herself:

—¡Y si viera usted qué bueno ha sido siempre!... ¡Cuánto nos quería!

No tenía más que un defecto, y es que nunca se contentaba con su suerte, sino que aspiraba a más, a más...

...Él mismo lo decía: 'Yo tengo que llegar a donde debo llegar, o me volveré loco.' (IV. 972–3)

Isidora's downfall will also be due to her untempered aspirations. Another indication of her future dilemma is her lack of common sense, so very typical of the Spain depicted in the *Novelas contemporáneas* of Galdós. She praises Rufete: 'Y no es que no trabajase...Iba a la oficina casi todos los días y se pasaba en ella lo menos dos horas' (IV. 972). She, like her father, will never be capable of doing a full day's work, and neither will she know that this is a failing. The use of 'casi' and 'lo menos' underlines Isidora's impractical views and increases the humorous effect of such a statement.

The confidential nature of these memories of her father lead Isidora to hint at her obsession: 'El que llamo mi padre fué más listo que el que llamo mi abuelo' (IV. 973). This brief allusion might have remained unemphasized by Isidora (who later returns to calling Rufete her father), if Canencia had not referred to her as 'noble criatura' (IV. 973). This ironic apostrophe sends Isidora into her deluded, egotistical musings: '—Y todo cuanto he padecido ha sido injusto— añadió ella prontamente, sorbiendo también una regular porción de aire, porque todo es contagioso en este mundo—. No sé si...Yo soy...' (IV, pp. 973–4). Isidora gulps air because Canencia has done so earlier. As the narrator comments, all is contagious – even demented tendencies. The fanatical aspect of both Isidora's behavior and her aspirations is brought home as Canencia takes the words out of her mouth to describe her 'noble' plight as a disinherited orphan who pertains to a much more elevated social class than her putative father, Rufete. The implications of this passage are multiple: an insane man recognizes Isidora's situation before she reveals it herself; hence those who believe in its truth may be as mad as Canencia. It is also a literary commonplace which serves as a commentary on Isidora's quest, and on *La deseheredada* as a whole. Yet if the reader fails to recognize such early qualifications of Isidora's character as the ambiguous references to her 'nobility', or the contagion of Canencia's demented symptoms, or the scribe's pseudo-prophetic intuition, he will become as much a victim of Isidora's warped vision of life as she is.

Isidora's immediate reaction to Canencia's 'wisdom' suggests the qualities of her character associated with her illusion, namely ignorance, vanity, pride, and a preoccupation with social convention: '¡De

qué manera tan clara relampagueó el orgullo en el semblante de
Isidora al oír aquellas palabras! Su rubor leve pasó pronto. Sus labios
vacilaron entre la sonrisa de vanidad y la denegación impuesta por las
conveniencias' (IV. 974). And she replies: '—Yo no quisiera hablar de
eso—dijo, tomando un tonillo enfático de calma y dignidad, que no
hacía buena concordancia con su ruso—' (IV. 974). The narrator
points out the disparity of her dress with her tone, which is a device he
uses frequently; when Isidora considers herself most refined or noble,
he deliberately recalls the incongruities of her situation. The comic
effect of her reply is highlighted by the use of the diminutive, 'tonillo',
which implies a condescending sense of superiority. Finishing her
sketch of Rufete, she once again describes herself: ' ¡Dios de mi vida!
Como él no tenía más idea que aparentar, aparentar, y ser persona
notable...' (IV. 974). And Canencia's summary of Rufete's error is
also Isidora's:

> —Hija mía —dijo el anciano con vivacidad—, una de las enfermedades
> del alma que más individuos trae a estas casas es la ambición, el afán de
> engrandecimiento, la envidia que los bajos tienen de los altos, y eso de
> querer subir atropellando a los que están arriba, no por la escalera del
> mérito y del trabajo, sino por la escala suelta de la intriga, o de la
> violencia, como si dijéramos, empujando, empujando...(IV. 974)

The significance of this passage for the entire novel is clear: Canencia
describes the ambition and envy which infects the souls of both Rufete
and Isidora. The image of the stairway (which appeared already in
Rufete's mutterings) will ultimately found the *moraleja* of the entire
novel: 'Si sentís anhelo de llegar a una difícil y escabrosa altura, no os
fiéis de las alas postizas. Procurad echarlas naturales, y en caso de que
no lo consigáis, pues hay infinitos ejemplos que confirman la negativa,
lo mejor, creedme, lo mejor será que toméis una escalera' (IV. 1162).

After summarizing the malady which is at the same time Rufete's,
Isidora's, and, he implies, much of Spain's, Canencia proceeds to reveal
his own insanity. Isidora absent-mindedly contemplates the objects in
the room, an exercise which foreshadows her future materialistic
fixations, at the same time as her guesses about the function of various
scholarly objects reveal her lack of formal education. Meanwhile,
Canencia's agitated discourse builds up to an irrational outburst. The
frightened Isidora is soon calmed by the director, who enters to inform
her of her father's death. As the grief-stricken heroine leaves the asylum
with Augusto Miquis, a childhood neighbor and now a medical
student, the narrator concludes his remarks on the inmates of Leganés

and their proximity to the reader's world. Once again he observes how thin a line separates reason from madness: 'Salieron Isidora y Augusto de la morada de la sinrazón y se alejaron silenciosos del tristísimo pueblo, en el cual casi todas las casas albergan dementes' (IV. 977). A last ironic observation is made concerning Isidora. In spite of her 'inconsolable grief' she has the presence of mind to keep up appearances; she carefully hides her broken boots beneath her skirt so Miquis will not see them. Such comments, like the others noted in this first chapter of *La desheredada*, are common throughout the novel: the narrator belies a positive or 'natural' sentiment (here grief) by calling attention to a simultaneous and compromising thought or action (here vanity). Such ironic juxtapositions may be either immediate or slightly delayed, and thus more likely to deceive the reader.

This analysis of the first chapter of *La desheredada* reveals how Galdós employs various means to focus on the novel's irony. It is typical of Galdós' technique to present the major elements at work in a character portrayal during the character's introduction, and then to elaborate on them throughout the novel. The introduction of Isidora demonstrates how her qualities of beauty, generosity, and love are compromised by her vain and proud pretensions. The indications of her conceit restrict the sympathy and compassion she might arouse in the reader because of her humble and uneducated station. Her basic irony consists of an inability to view herself and others the way the narrator, the other characters, and the reader do. Some of the ways in which her ironic position is revealed are: self-characterization, when Isidora believes she is describing only someone else; an inability to judge situations and people accurately, which reveals a lack of insight or shallowness; modes of interaction with others – and herself – in which the external and internal aspects of her personality are seen as contradictory; and an idealized self-conception.

The text often displays ironically juxtaposed images, events, speech, thoughts, or characters. These juxtapositions may be quite subtle, such as the introduction of Isidora following a discussion of the *locas*. Or they may be more explicit, such as the contrast noted between her dignified tone and her humble attire. Most frequently these ironies result from peculiarities of word choice or sentence structure, or from the whole sequence of sentences. Oddly placed subordinate clauses, unusual applications of the diminutive or pejorative, repetition, and other stylistic indicators, though not extravagant, still attract the reader's attention to the value of the elements that they appose.[10]

The use of the free indirect style allows the reader to view Isidora's subjective musings with familiarity and often with sympathy. The free indirect style facilitates changes in narrative voice and allows for various degrees of irony when Isidora's sentiments are incongruent with the situation. This 'play of voices' between irony and sympathy, narrator and character, offers different perspectives on the narrative, conflicting interpretations, which are the essence of irony. The narrator may also appropriate isolated words or ideas from Isidora's vocabulary into his own discourse in a parodic or exaggerated manner in order to emphasize her distinct view of herself and society. Dialogue, too, can lead to irony in certain situations. Dialogue appears to separate the narrator from the character and allows her to unwittingly be her own ironist. The narrator frequently assumes a stance away from Isidora so that she herself reveals the depths (or shallows) of her personality. This gesture facilitates the broader relationship of irony which the novel projects – the possibility of the reader's naive participation. Iser has pointed out that the greater the distance which the narrator takes from a character, the closer the reader is enabled to move: 'The actual gap between the character's actions and the narrator's comments stimulates the reader into forming judgments of his own' (p. 108). The judgment may be that of the reader skilled in recognizing the text's ironic *vraisemblance*, or that of the naive 'quixotic' reader. Such induced participation in the ambiguities and enigmas of the text increases the possibility that the reader will be ironized. Isidora is, as already indicated, not without a sympathetic side, nor is the case of her relationship to the Marquesa clear. This ambiguity contributes to the suspense of the story and prohibits Isidora from becoming a negative ironic stereotype, just as irony prevents her from becoming a romantic cliché.

The introduction of Isidora is clearly an important component of her characterization; equally important are the relationships established between herself and the other characters in the novel. There is a specular relationship between the portrait of Isidora and the novel as a whole, just as there is between Cervantes' parodies of the chivalric novel (and its public) and the novel *Don Quijote*. Moreover, the structure of this relationship and others in *La desheredada* reflects those in *Don Quijote*, often in a distorted or parodic manner. Isidora does not recognize the character that others see in her, and sees individuals like herself without recognizing herself in them. The juxtaposition of Isidora's character to others may function as either an opposition or an apposition, that is, either a contrast or a comparison. In the former, it is the dissimilarity, in the latter, the similarity, between Isidora and another character which offers the reader an opportunity to understand each of them better. Some juxtapositions between Isidora and other characters include elements of both opposition and apposition, as in the case of Canencia. His apparent wisdom and paternal air are apposed to Isidora's naiveté and mask his insanity; yet his conversation with Isidora reveals the fanatically vain presumption which lies beneath her humble façade and is apposed to his own delusions. Such juxtapositions play more important roles when Isidora is compared to the other characters in the novel. An analysis of these relationships exposes further, latent levels of specularity.

The first character to be ironically juxtaposed to Isidora after her introduction is her aunt, *la Sanguijuelera*. A vulgar and uneducated but honest shopkeeper, she is both a reflection of and a commentary on her niece. The episode begins with a less than favorable digression on the somewhat aberrant psychology of Isidora, whom the narrator still insists on calling, 'por respeto a la rutina, hija de Rufete' (IV. 977). The reader learns that Isidora customarily strives to imagine every detail of an event hours, even days, before it occurs, and has a 'manía' – a term which implicitly recalls Leganés – for exaggerating her impressions of things. This account of her mental processes renders intensely parodic the narrator's subsequent deference to Isidora's pretensions in the words 'Isidora se había figurado que su tía – o más bien, tía de su supuesta madre' (IV. 978), where the verb 'figurar' indicates her over-vivid imagination at work. In the *costumbrista* sketch of the locale the narrator immediately tells us that the shop contains a 'miserable ajuar de cacharros ordinarios' (IV. 978). But as the description through Isidora's eyes continues in the free indirect style, the habitation assumes a more favorable appearance. Isidora, who could not bear the disgrace of even a putative relative's vulgarity, salvages an impression of propriety by telling herself that the shop is at least neat and clean.

As in Leganés, Isidora is at first a sympathetic character; she embraces her aunt, crying. Her dismay (although impractical) that her brother, Mariano, works in a rope factory instead of attending school seems naturally based on love and a concern for his welfare. After the description of Isidora's pensive attitude during the meal, the reader is invited to ponder what she is thinking, since the narrator feigns ignorance: 'Parecía que estaba atormentada de una idea' (IV. 983). Her torment is the *idée fixe* of the moment and of the entire novel. Then, 'Como quien se quita una máscara, Isidora dejó su aspecto de sumisa mansedumbre, y en tono resuelto pronunció estas palabras:...' (IV. 983). The simile defines the facility with which she plays roles. As Isidora tells her aunt that she and her brother are not Rufete's children, believing that *la Sanguijuelera* already knows this, the old woman becomes furious. She realizes that most of Isidora's ideas have been acquired in novels, and the specularity is emphatic: 'Me parece que tú te has hartado de leer esos librotes que llaman novelas. ¡Cuánto mejor es no saber leer! Mírate en mi espejo' (IV. 984). Even an illiterate woman recognizes the romantic commonplaces. And the further irony here is that Isidora will not or cannot ever see clearly in the mirror of parentage and truth, or in any other. Isidora's affectation, so obviously literary, is revealed: '—Mi madre —declaró Isidora, poniéndose la mano en el corazón para comprimir, sin duda, un movimiento afectuoso demasiasiado vivo—, mi madre...fué hija de una marquesa' (IV. 984). (The insertion of 'sin duda' casts doubt on her sincerity rather than illustrating her affection. The use of the phrase frequently calls attention to irony. An excellent example of this occurs after one of her shopping trips during which she has spent nearly all of her money on trifling luxuries. In enumerating these assorted items, the narrator remarks: 'Más necesario era, sin duda, el librito de memorias, el plano de Madrid, las cinco novelas y la jaula, aunque todavía le faltaba el pájaro' (IV. 1044).) With this first clear revelation of just who Isidora thinks she is – the granddaughter of a *marquesa* – there is a foreshadowing of her end. *La Sanguijuelera* tries to beat some sense into her and Isidora falls upon the dirt floor (physically lower than her aunt). From this posture, Isidora attempts to insult her sarcastically: '¡Cómo se conoce —dijo al fin la sobrina con vivísimo tono de desprecio— que no es usted persona decente!' (IV. 985). Her aunt replies: '¡Más que tú...!' Both statements are true, but Isidora cannot understand them. When judged by the standards of decency and honor which pertain to their particular social class, *la Sanguijuelera* will rise far above her niece. Before Isidora's final fall into an ignominious state of prostitution among the lowest depths of society, her aunt offers to make Isidora her heiress and to take her into the shop. But Isidora rejects this and better offers. Now as she flees the neighborhood amid jeers and stares she exclaims in the closing sentence of the chapter: '¡Qué odioso, qué soez, qué repugnante es el pueblo!' Isidora despises the very *pueblo* identity which she herself truly possesses. The importance of Isidora's rejection of the *pueblo* is emphasized by its position in the last sentence of the chapter. Disposition is clearly a pervasive tool of irony in Galdós' art.

Augusto Miquis' prominent position in the novel is foretold by his fortuituous entrance at the end of chapter I. He will be the antithesis to Isidora in many ways. He is intelligent and level-headed, honorable and humble; we see, moreover, that he has a profound sense of irony. Isidora's continual rejection of him and his good advice metonymically represents her rejection of honor and practicality. Miquis' brash appearance masks a modest self-concept, while Isidora's humble exterior conceals a profound arrogance. Isidora's attitude toward Miquis is overlaid with an egotism that precludes her seeing his superior moral character and intellect. Her principal reason for rejecting him is his social position; only too late, when she finally views him from the depths of her depravity, does she realize the moral and social heights she could have reached with him.

In chapter IV the narrator provides us with more details of the heroine's background as he did before the episode with *la Sanguijuelera*. Iser (p. 108) has noted that this type of privileged information usually distances the reader from the character, allowing him to see her imbalance. Again Isidora's fantastic imagination is described; her fantasies allow her to lead an apocryphal life that comes to supplant her reality. Her maniacal tendencies are invoked with the designation 'enfermizo trabajo' (IV. 986). The parallel to the *Quijote* is obvious in the use of the historical chronicle device which occasionally appears, as in 'los documentos de que se ha formado esta historia' (IV. 986). This is a parodical allusion because the chronicle is used to describe her boots. As she dresses for her outing with Miquis, she vainly contemplates how attractive her small feet are in the new boots. The dual 'irreality' of the scene is confirmed in her decision to give the old boots to the 'primer pobre que a la puerta llegase' (IV. 986), not realizing how poor she is herself. Isidora's 'fictions' are reflected in the ways the novel as a whole constantly calls attention to its own fictions, in this instance through reference to the Cervantine chronicle.[11]

The reality of Isidora's social station is fundamental to her irony and is emphasized again in chapter IV through her fixation on the concept of *pueblo*. As she gazes admiringly upon the masterpieces in the Prado with Miquis, her apparently natural appreciation for great art is immediately belied by her consideration of the public: 'Preguntó a Miquis si también en aquel sitio destinado a albergar lo sublime dejaban entrar al pueblo, y como el estudiante le contestara que sí, se asombró mucho de ello' (IV. 987). A similar technique is used to spoil the effect of her compassion for the caged animals in the Retiro: '—Esto es espectáculo para el pueblo —dijo con desdén—. Vámonos de aquí' (IV. 990). She is also repulsed by the little open-air restaurant to which Miquis takes her. She rejects her own origins in the *pueblo*, yet classifies as 'para el pueblo' the spectacles and attractions in which she herself participates.

Isidora has conventional, even vulgarized, notions of what proper aristocratic attitudes are, and these shape her arrogance. As she walks with Miquis through the Buen Retiro, Isidora suppresses her natural response, 'instintos de independencia y de candoroso salvajismo', in order to contemplate the passers-by. She quickly adapts herself to what she believes is proper behavior:

Prontamente se acostumbró el espíritu de ella a considerar el Retiro... como una ingeniosa adaptación de la Naturaleza a la cultura: comprendió que el hombre, que ha domesticado a las bestias, ha sabido también civilizar al bosque. Echando, pues, de su alma aquellos vagos deseos de correr y columpiarse, pensó gravemente de este modo: 'Para otra vez que venga, traeré yo mis guantes y mi sombrilla.' (IV. 987)

The passage from thoughtful contemplation to banal obsession with appearances is humorously underscored by the adverb 'gravemente'. The absurdity of her attitude is made abundantly clear when Miquis directs her attention to the song of a nightingale:

Isidora había oído hablar de los ruiseñores como cifra y resumen de toda la poesía de la Naturaleza; pero no los había oído. Estos artistas no iban nunca por la Mancha. Puso atención, creyendo oír odas y canciones, y su semblante expresaba un éxtasis melancólico, aunque a decir verdad lo que se oía era una conversación de miles de picos, un galimatías parlamentario-forestal, donde el músico más sutil no podría encontrar las endechas amorosas de que tanto se ha abusado en literatura. (IV. 987–8)

The elaborate literary language which constitutes portions of both passages is obviously not Isidora's; the verbose expressions ironize both her uneducated discourse (which is juxtaposed to them), and their own status as literary cliché.

So far Isidora's ignorance has not been condemned emphatically. The narrative tone becomes especially negative, however, as Isidora reveals more of herself. She wonders at the beauty of the Cosmos and expresses a desire to learn: ' ¡El Cosmos! ¡Qué bonito eco tuvo esta palabra en la mente de Isidora! ¡Cuánto daría por saber qué era aquello del Cosmos!...porque verdaderamente ella deseaba y necesitaba instruirse' (IV. 989). This is entirely Isidora's discourse, in marked contrast to the previous quotations. Here her lack of education is also obvious, yet there is a difference; in this passage the free indirect style is uncontaminated by the narrator's intrusions of sophisticated language.[12] Isidora's naive, but apparently sincere proposal to educate herself may attract the reader's sympathy. But later, after a prolonged dialogue with Miquis, her fundamental attitude toward learning emerges: '—Yo no quiero ser sabia, vamos, sino saber lo preciso, lo que saben todas las personas de la buena sociedad, un poquito, una idea de todo...¿me entiendes?' (IV. 990). The conventional pretense to topical but shallow knowledge is satirized here. The reader's own susceptibility to this social satire lies in the possibility that he agrees with the convention.

In the last two sections of the chapter Isidora's innate haughtiness is emphasized. Without realizing the seriousness of his words, Miquis calls Isidora 'marquesa' and lauds the 'noble pueblo' which is everyone's origin. (Note the irony of 'noble pueblo' from Isidora's perspective.) Isidora listens impatiently to his little speech. He compounds his error by mentioning a distant relative who works in the Aransis palace that is owned by the family to which Isidora believes she belongs. Although she is shaken, her reaction is a controlled one: 'Al oír este nombre Isidora, palideció, y el corazón saltó en el pecho. Su espontaneidad quiso decir algo; pero se contuvo, asustada de las indiscreciones que podría cometer' (IV. 992). She alludes to a brighter future for herself, but does not tell Miquis her whole 'story'.

Isidora's budding disdain for Miquis involves more than pride; it assumes a certain hypocrisy. As they exchange tender words of endearment it is clear to the reader that she contemplates their relationship in terms of his future fame. He mockingly asks if she will remember him when she attains a higher social position; she replies: '—¿Pues no me he de acordar? Serás entonces un médico célebre' (IV. 993). They touch hands emotionally and 'Isidora volvió a pensar en que nunca más saldría a la calle sin guantes' (IV. 993). Her banal concern with appearances is a subtle reminder to the reader of her egotism. Their frolic in the Retiro is interrupted when Isidora sees the coaches passing on the Castellana, and their differing perspectives on society become explicit: 'Miquis veía lo que todo el mundo ve;...Pero Isidora...vió algo más de lo que vemos todos' (IV. 994). The 'algo más' which she sees is elegance and beauty, rather than tackiness and pretense. Her ecstatic contemplation and praise of this spectacle are partially related in the free indirect style, permitting the reader a full view of her intoxication. She asks Miquis why he does not ride a horse too; he replies that he considers it *cursi*, and she abuses him with derogatory names. Isidora refuses to accept the applicability of this term whose repeated use in the novel corresponds to its social and personal import for the self-concept of Galdós' reader. Tierno Galván suggests that the spectacle of *cursilería* necessarily provokes an ironic rebellion in one who observes it, because it 'descubre el fondo común del que ambos participan'. The degree of rebellion depends upon the degree of community which the observer feels with the *cursi* person, and manifests itself most forcefully as pity for a person who, though like oneself, has incurred the most ignominious of indiscretions.[13]

Precisely because she does not consider herself to be like others, Isidora ignores Miquis' legitimate condemnation of the farce, pretension, and hypocrisy of the passing high society which is often – unknown to Isidora – far in debt. She is as unaware of their actual circumstances as she is of her own. Enthralled with their appearance of grandeur, she scorns Miquis' proposal of marriage:

—¡Si yo no me caso contigo!...—declaró la joven en un momento de espontaneidad.
Había en su expresión un tonillo de lástima impertinente, que poco más o menos quería decir: '¡Si yo soy mucho para ti, tan pequeño!' (IV. 995)

The diminutive defines the petty condescension of her remark. Her partial rejection of Miquis becomes complete and permanent as she arrives home to find a calling-card left her. The next chapter introduces her to the owner of the card, 'El marqués viudo de Saldeoro', Joaquín Pez, whom she believes to be her first step up the ladder to honor and nobility. Actually he will be her first step down, as she leaves behind her best chance of honor and esteem with Miquis.

Joaquín Pez holds forth to Isidora (and the reader) the prospect of her nobility and the hope of success, because he seems to take her claim to the Aransis house seriously. He becomes the first in a series of progressively more despicable lovers, seducing Isidora with money and gentlemanly affectations. His shallowness never becomes apparent to Isidora, who is first attracted by the glamour of his title. Joaquín is like Isidora in so many ways that she fails to recognize her reflection in him, and is insulted when he labels her for what she is. In the anticlimactic scene before her seduction, she reacts to the overtures with which

Joaquín expresses his true designs in a way that reveals her slight moral consciousness. Because her funds have been exhausted, he offers her more money, along with the hope of soon winning recognition. She barely curbs her excitement at the sight of the money when she realizes that Joaquín is trying to buy her. She is not morally indignant, but rather proud:

Rápidamente conoció Isidora la proximidad de su mal, y tuvo una de esas inspiraciones de dignidad y honor que son propias en las naturalezas no gastadas. Su debilidad tuvo por defensor y escudo al sentimiento que, por otra parte, era causa de todos sus males: el orgullo. Se salvó por su defecto, así como otros se salvan por su mérito. No es fácil definir lo que rápidamente pensó, las cosas que trajo a la memoria, las sacudidas que dió a su dignidad de Aransis para que se despertase y saliese a defenderla (IV. 1041)

The irony of her reaction could not be more evident; it is doubly incisive because she in fact possesses no such 'dignidad de Aransis'. She easily forgives Joaquín – for his written apology is accompanied by bank notes – but not his insulting denomination, 'cursilona'.

Agradeció ella con toda su alma el desagravio, y sus aflicciones de aquel día se le disiparon con la grata vista del pan bendito, o llámase papel-moneda. Dió al olvido sus agravios; pero si perdonó fácilmente a Joaquín la injuria intentada contra su honor, tuvo que hacer un esfuerzo de bondad para perdonarle el que le hubiera llamado cursilona. Tal es la condición humana, que a veces el rasguño hecho al amor propio duele más que la puñalada asestada contra la honra. (IV. 1041)

This moment illustrates two of the signal characteristics which Tierno Galván attributes to lo cursi: ignorance and weakness ('Lo cursi', passim). Isidora ignores this gross offense to her chastity and displays incurable weakness for money.

The narrative's increasing emphasis of Isidora's venality is highlighted by the metaphor 'pan bendito'. At one point she describes her ideal life to Joaquín; the order of elements is revealing: 'Riqueza, mucha riqueza; una montaña de dinero; luego otra montaña de honradez, y al mismo tiempo una montaña, una cordillera de amor legítimo' (IV. 1092). Her need for wealth is eventually an even stronger driving force than her desire for nobility, and in the final chapters she barters her remaining honor for money. This aspect of her personality is again 'reflected' through a mirror. Before finally selling herself into a life of prostitution, she takes one last look in a broken mirror, and the image she sees is purely monetary: 'Todavía soy guapa...y cuando

me reponga seré guapísima. Valgo mucho, y valdré muchísimo más'
(IV. 1159). The irony of these lines is that she seems to be using only
one definition of 'valer' – monetary worth; she has lost all sense of
personal merit. Her refusal to be ordinary has led her along the same
path as many ordinary poor girls – to common prostitution.

In Isidora's and Joaquín's last scene together, which occurs long
after he has abandoned her and his child to other lovers, the specularity
of their spendthrift, impractical, and self-deluded personalities becomes
most apparent. After squandering his fortune and falling deeply in
debt he comes again to Isidora for help. Their meeting is presented
entirely in dialogue, which enables both characters to expose their self-
deception without interruption. Isidora's remark about the stairs as she
enters the room ironically describes her own path: ' ¡Dios mío, qué
escalera!' (IV. 1120). She ascends the stairs physically while descending
morally, an opposition which is a narrative and a cultural irony. The
lowest strata of the novelistic society live in the highest places. Isidora
still believes she is ascending socially; she speaks in this scene of the
impending victory of her court claim only minutes (or sentences) before
she is arrested for presenting forged documents. The expensive meal
which Isidora orders with the few *duros* she still possesses underscores
the impracticality of their values. Joaquín's and Isidora's apparent
praise of each other is simply self-admiration. As she discusses her taste
for classical music, of which she is almost totally ignorant, Joaquín
assures her that she is noble. She replies: 'Te diré. . . Oyendo aquella
música yo me olvidaba de todo y bendecía a Dios, que no me ha hecho
vulgo' (IV. 1123).[14] But she is as common as she is ignoble. She possesses
the same faults of egoism, fickleness, and materialism as are revealed in
Joaquín. He thinks of her before writing a letter that he believes will be
his last living act: 'Nuestras dos almas han simpatizado, porque son
similares. Tú, como yo, fuiste educada en la idea de igualar a los
superiores' (IV. 1125). We are reminded of the warning against the
dangers of such an education, contained in the *moraleja* of the novel,
where the image of the stairs and the theme of education come together.

While Joaquín Pez is Isidora's most effective mirror-image among
her lovers, others place in relief various important aspects of her personality. Sánchez Botín, an immensely rich, boorish hypocrite, brings out
Isidora's hypocrisy. She met him in a church where she was passing
time after having resolved to be honorable and work (at a job still not
decided upon, nor ever to be). The narrator is straightforward in this
description, which conveys a comment on the prevalence of shallow

piety. Her attention is held more by the other women (as well dressed as in the theater) whom she envies, than by the ritual. The narrator sarcastically comments that: 'La belleza de las postulantes aguza la caridad' (IV. 1076). Isidora's representative role prevents her from being condemned outright by the narrator here. Well-dressed charity and shallow piety are social conventions which she (and possibly the reader) has been taught to accept. Her ironic position as a naive though willing victim of social fiction is made analogous to that of Humanity in general. She joins in contemplating the constant eye-movement in the church as the parishioners, especially those of the opposite sex, observe each other. The description ends with the narrator's exclamation 'iMísera Humanidad!' (IV. 1077). Shortly afterwards Botín, the very man whom she had noticed staring at her, propositions her, presenting himself as 'un bienhechor de la Humanidad' (IV. 1077). This is highly ironical because the figure of Isidora postulates a Humanity whose devotion lies not on the path to heaven, but on the materialist way to hell. The salvation Botín offers is instead a luxurious temptation.

Botín's successor, Melchor Relimpio, offers another apposition, for Isidora had always detested his presumptions, although she is as *cursi* as he. The narrator describes him as one 'tan desnudo de saber como vestido de presunción', who believes that 'había de ser pronto un personaje, una notabilidad' (IV. 1015). Where Isidora had been led to believe in her noble descent, Melchor had been raised to believe in the distinguished superiority of his eminently undistinguished person. The result in each case is the same: Isidora's noble delusion is fed by folletinesque tales of estranged heirs finally united with their fortunes, while Melchor's sanguine self-confidence is nourished by café gossip – perhaps accepted by the reader himself – regarding miraculous metamorphoses from rags to riches. Nonetheless, Isidora's reaction to Melchor's expectations is entirely negative: 'Parecíale el más desaforado holgazán, el más bárbaro egoísta del mundo' (IV. 1022). The reader who is accustomed to the ironic tone of the novel cannot avoid applying some of these adjectives to Isidora. These words significantly conclude chapter VIII, while chapter IX begins with a reference to 'El palacio de Aransis' – a reminder of Isidora's own pretensions. Isidora's egotistical needs – particularly her addiction to beautiful clothing – eventually lead her to become Melchor's mistress.

Juan Bou ('ox' in Catalan), though born of common stock like Isidora, leads an honorable hard-working life, is satisfied with his lot and prosperous through decent means. Isidora refuses the Catalan printer's offer of marriage until it is too late, just as she refused to participate in his lottery ticket – which eventually won. Her rejection of Bou takes place in the palace of Aransis where her 'noble being' is in its element. She is indignant at the audacity of such an unworthy creature and nearly laughs in his face. But she does become his lover later in order to give money to Joaquín, who would never marry her. Bou finally loses interest because of her disdainful attitude, even while he has been paying her jail costs. Too late she decides that only marriage with him can save her.

She turns then to her last official lover, Gaitica, a sadistic thug from her brother Mariano's circle of depraved associates; like her, he claims to be a disinherited nobleman. He drags Isidora down with him to his level of depravity, just as he instigated her brother's final perdition. But she still maintains the pride which pushes her to be what she is not, 'por una inexplicable modificación de su orgullo, en parecer peor de lo que era' (IV. 1156). The decreasing social and moral stature of Isidora's successive lovers is an index for the reader of the decreasing plausibility of her noble aspirations.

The juxtaposition of Isidora to her brother Mariano forms an apparent opposition between their personalities, and a possible apposition of their genetic make-up. This adds a naturalistic element to Isidora's character: the suggestion that Mariano's simplemindedness and dementia are inherited has obvious implications for his sister. Even the contrast between their personalities diminishes near the end of the novel, however, when Isidora appropriates the vulgar language of her brother, which she had once condemned.

The reader attentive to these explicit or implicit transfers of features from one character to another will be able to extrapolate their development toward their probable conclusion. The portrait of Isidora reflects, in the permutations of its component features, the deployment of the symbolic, thematic, and cultural codes which form the text.

Even more complex than the juxtaposition of Isidora to other characters in the novel is the juxtaposition between the two Isidoras of *La desheredada* – the one seen by herself and the one seen by the reader. The double perspective has already been apparent in her dialogues with other characters, and even more in her thoughts about them, which, when expressed in the free indirect style, facilitate this dual view. Verdín has noted that 'Es muy frecuente en el estilo indirecto libre el desdoblamiento de la personalidad: personaje que habla y personaje que piensa, que se pregunta y que se responde como si se tratase de dos "yo" distintos' (p. 92). When Isidora ponders her nobility, her distorted image of herself is especially visible. 'Free indirect style also provides a natural vehicle for reveries, lyrical effusions and self-analysis', Ullman observes, and 'Thanks to the free indirect method, the internal monologue can develop into a kind of internal dialogue' (*Style in the French Novel*, p. 113). The role which Isidora's imagination plays as the cause of her problems is emphasized by the extensive narration devoted to her day-dreams and fantasies. Much of this is given in interior monologues, where the largest number of *doubles entendres* occur. Chapter xi is dedicated solely to her insomniac musings during the night after her first visit to the (then empty) Aransis palace. Her anticipation of the yet to be arranged meeting with her 'grandmother' is disturbed by her worries about the proper dress: 'Temo presentarme a mi abuela con esta facha innoble... Tanta vergüenza tengo de mí, que quisiera no hubiese espejos en el mundo' (IV. 1030). But she is not noble, and the shame she feels before the mirror now is the inverse of her sentiment later when, covered with indecency, she wears fine clothing. The reasons she gives for her insomnia are ironically true: 'Esto me vuelve loca' (IV. 1030); 'Yo tengo algo, yo estoy enferma. Este latido, este sacudimiento no es natural' (IV. 1031). 'En mi cabeza hay algo que no marcha bien. Esto es una enfermedad' (IV. 1032). In planning her behavior toward Joaquín she forecasts the scene in which he tries to buy her: 'Conviene tener dignidad. ¿Soy, acaso, como esas cursis que se enamoran del primero que llega? No, en mi clase no se rinde el corazón sin defenderse' (IV. 1032). Joaquín is in fact her second admirer, Miquis was the first. By refusing the label *cursi* for herself, Isidora refuses to see the common basis of her real and illusory selves. To admit that she might be *cursi* would be to deny her nobility. Rather than accept her likeness to others, she aspires to another life. The reader who condemns Isidora will find himself in the uncomfortable position of saying 'I am not like this person, who thinks she is not like anyone else.'

In a later chapter entitled 'Anagnórisis' she prepares for the actual meeting with her 'grandmother' and considers her future position: 'Era preciso que en su apariencia comedida, modesta, honrada y grave revelara la dignidad con que pasaba de su estado miserable a otro esplendoroso' (IV. 1052). But the reader has seen that Isidora is anything but modest and grave, and there is scarcely any dignity of Aransis for her. She is obsessed, seeing not reality, but her illusion in the mirror: 'Su dignidad, su hermosura, su derecho mismo, resplandecían más en la decencia correcta y limpia de su vestido negro' (IV. 1052). This use of the free indirect style (indicated especially by 'derecho mismo') might be confusing, for although her grandmother rejects her, there is still doubt about what the Marquesa actually thinks. Thus, for the reader who believes as Isidora does, the preceding passage might be attributed to the narrator's view of Isidora's right and resplendent dignity, rather than to her own self-conception. The passage lends a high degree of uncertainty to the question 'who is speaking?' This 'play of voices' observable in the free indirect style allows one voice gently to dissolve into another without warning. This contributes to what Barthes praises as the 'plurality of the text'.[15]

The ambiguity surrounding Isidora's claim to nobility begins with Rufete's dying words, and concludes with those written by her *tío canónigo* in his death-bed letter to Isidora at the conclusion of Part I. For if the last words of a man are conventionally taken to be the 'truth', as are those of Don Quijote, then the parodic significance of this novel reaches its zenith in the hackneyed clichés which her uncle, who only fancies himself a *canónigo*, offers as truths. Where Isidora recalls Don Quijote, her uncle, an extravagantly eccentric 'loco–cuerdo' named Santiago Quijano-Quijada, is almost the knight of La Mancha himself. Similarly, where the parody of *La desheredada* recalls that of *Don Quijote*, it asserts the closest of intertextual relations with Cervantes' work. The last letter of Isidora's uncle is a pastiche of dime novel banalities. To the quixotic reader – an Isidora or a consumer of the *folletín* – such language is realistic, if not reality itself. To the critical reader it displays the ironic problematics of the novel as fiction. Not only is *La desheredada* a parody of *Don Quijote* and of the *folletín*, but it is also an ironic comment on itself and on all literature. In its gesture toward the 'real' world, the novel destroys its own claim to reality; it proclaims the unbridgeable distance between language and being, fiction and reality.

Throughout Part I the narrator has encouraged the quixotic reader as a means of increasing the force of his final *desengaño*. The constant use of aporia, ambiguity, and enigma fosters this duplicitous reading. Thus, Isidora's naturally 'noble' appreciation of beauty is frequently mentioned, and not always with overt irony; in fact she is often praised straightforwardly for her positive attributes. When she sees a portrait of Virginia de Aransis, she is left 'muerta de asombro y amor' (IV. 1030) as she recognizes the similarity to herself. Even her uncle, José

Relimpio, claims that 'he has seen that face before'. If these two characters' opinions are not to be trusted, what about that of the Marquesa? In her interview with Isidora she admits a physical likeness to her daughter, although she rejects Isidora's claim. Nonetheless, the Marquesa seems 'turbada', before Isidora leaves, and the narrator asks, '¿Cruzó por la mente de la noble señora un rayo de duda?... ¿Vaciló su firme creencia? ¡Quién puede saberlo! A sus ojos asomaron las lágrimas' (iv. 1055). The reader, forewarned about the Marquesa's Calderonian sense of honor, might suppose that she has another – though still literary – reason for rejecting Isidora. Even in Part ii, the narrator refers at one point without obvious irony to Isidora's son as 'el Sucesor de los Rufetes (o Aransis, que ello está por saber)' (iv. 1071). The narrator's misleading insinuations to the reader contribute as much to advancing the plot as Isidora's attorney's reassurances of legal victory. Just as Isidora prefers to believe the word of her lawyer against all evidence to the contrary, so a quixotic reader might prefer to accept literally only the tritest elements of *folletín* romance from the narration, rather than submit them to the text's ironic *vraisemblance*.

It is Miquis – the voice of truth and of irony, as the narrator often indicates – along with his father-in-law, who finally convinces Isidora that she has been the victim of a charade. She reflects on the sentimental education which she received in her youth, and finally loses her faith and her identity, of which 'no quedaba en su alma sino una grande y disolvente ironía' (iv. 1151). Miquis' ironical voice of truth, like Isidora's realization of the ironical truth of her life, point toward the conclusion that the essence of truth is irony.

The totality of Isidora's irony approaches a cosmic level, which is emphasized in the words 'grande y disolvente'. It is a multiple irony because that identity which she believes she has lost never existed, except as a fictional construction. As she loses her illusions at last, she comes as close as she ever does to seeing herself, and to having an identity. But this moment of truth is fleeting and Isidora soon subjects herself to the fiction of a life more 'ignoble' than that in Tomelloso. Her consequent disappearance from the society of the novel signifies the totality of her absence even from her own fiction, and of the distance of that fiction from the world. Unlike Zola, Galdós will not 'follow' her further. Isidora incorporates the negation of meaning that irony ultimately describes.

The portrait of Rosalía de Bringas, like that of Isidora Rufete, offers a mordant commentary on Spanish society in Galdós' time.[16] It moves to ironize the reader as a participant in society and its conventions, and as a consumer of literary fictions. Like Isidora, Rosalía is a conjunction of all the ironic intertextualities in her novel; the construct of her character cannot be isolated from the novel's complex of literary, cultural, and symbolic codes. The portrait derives from, at the same time as it lends meaning to, the other codes in the narrative. The literary, cultural, and symbolic connotations within these codes, their discrete semes, also reach beyond the novel toward the world where they have functional value or significance. In effect, this intertextuality of word and world forms the very medium through which Rosalía and her irony can be read. For a novelistic character becomes ironic only by displaying as ironic the codes of thought and convention through which the reader approaches the text. This process, in which the conventions that enable a meaningful reading are themselves ironized, can be especially well illustrated in an analysis of Rosalía. The dominant conventions of the novelistic society in which she moves, and which the reader recognizes as similar to his own, are the vehicles of their own irony.

The portrait of Rosalía in *La de Bringas* elaborates upon her presentation in *Tormento*. This development from a secondary character to the leading character in a novel of her own name is a revealing process in Galdós' art (although, as Clarín first aptly noted, Rosalía is already in *Tormento* almost more of a protagonist than Amparo or Agustín). For the irony of Rosalía in *Tormento* is different from that in *La de Bringas*, just as the irony in both of these novels differs from that in *La desheredada*. A comparative reading of these three characterizations will illustrate more clearly the effectiveness of some of the techniques already discussed. The same narrative devices which are at work in *La desheredada* creating an ironic portrait of Isidora are present in Rosalía's two novels. In the case of Rosalía, the irony-creating functions of these devices are alternately suppressed and exaggerated. These stylistic modifications change the over-all tone and force of the portrait.

Rosalía is a much more satirical figure than Isidora. Her portrait is somewhat one-sided in *Tormento*, but a subtler irony makes it more problematic in *La de Bringas*. The realization of this satiric bent in the narrative sheds more light on Galdós' didactic and stylistic methods, as well as on their interrelation. Because satiric irony, or 'corrective irony', tends to be more 'intentional and didactic', its use in these novels is especially fitting; both are pointed criticisms of Galdós' own society.[17] Even more than Isidora, the figure of Rosalía is offered up to the reader as an example of his own possible weaknesses and follies. Her obsession with appearances – at the expense of a more realistic and frank approach to life – is particularly bourgeois. Her generally shallow attitude toward politics, religion, and nobility may parallel that of many readers. The Isabelline society in which her parasitic personality thrives is not very distant in years or manners from the reader's world of the 1880s, and the similarities are explicit. Rosalía's 'real' desires, in contrast to the 'fictional' illusions of Isidora, make her presumption and materialism even more condemnable. Because she is a more clearly negative figure, and her portrait more satirical, the reader more easily avoids identification with Rosalía individually; yet because the ambiguity and sympathy intimated in *La desheredada* are largely absent from *La de Bringas*, the negative associations with the reader's society become more direct. Instead of a prolonged process of re-evaluation, which provides a lesson in reading as well, the portrait of Rosalía offers an immediate opportunity for the reader's criticism. There is little mistaking the moral and social commentary implicit in her characterization which the attention to detail in the description of her makes all the more effective. The minute descriptions of her home, clothing, facial expressions, intonations, and gestures allow the reader almost to visualize her existence. Such details, often otherwise insignificant, permit the reader to believe that he is dealing with the '*réel*'.[18] The sense of familiarity which accompanies this may give a false feeling of security; for a world so 'real' in its material detail may also include equally 'real' moral and social deficiencies.

Like Isidora, Rosalía is ironized through the exposition of her apparent virtues. She unconsciously describes herself when categorizing others. She affects a naive self-concept, which the reader penetrates. Her pretensions are explicitly belied by the commentary of the narrator, or rationalized for an even subtler ironic effect. The narrative modes which facilitate this irony are again the free indirect style, interior monologue, and dialogue – including theatrically dramatized dialogues. The narrator's asides, unusual or emphatic word-placements, double meanings, inversion, diminutives and pejoratives, and other stylistic devices identify the ironic tone. The more subtly the narrator insinuates his comments and the more imperceptibly narrative voices shift, the more problematic the irony becomes and the more uncertain the reader feels. Thus the search to uncover the 'true meaning', to naturalize an ironic *vraisemblance*, is intensified. The reader's increased participation in the text further contributes to a realization of its irony.

Rosalía is less problematic to the reader in *Tormento* in part because little sympathy is shown for her by the narrator; the satirical attitude is explicit. However, the goal of such satire must still be discovered by the reader at whom it is aimed. Rosalía is depicted from the beginning as wholly vain and proud, and there is nothing illusory about her noble pretensions. Her scheming cruelty to the beautiful orphan heroine of the novel, Amparo, precludes any pity for her own disappointments. The most important difference between the presentation of Rosalía in *Tormento* and the presentations of Isidora and the later Rosalía is the greater distance that is maintained between the character and the reader. As Ronald Paulson and others have pointed out, this is one effect of satire.[19] Rosalía is not allowed to present herself directly to the reader as frequently as Isidora is, a feature of the novel which is obvious from the outset. Isidora's own discourse introduced her in the first chapter of *La desheredada* through the free indirect style and then dialogue. Any 'historical' information was reserved for later chapters, and the background was not complete until her own reveries in jail brought her to reflect on her youth. In *Tormento*, however, Rosalía is presented through a more historical mode of narration which occupies nearly all of chapters II and III before she is allowed to speak. The distance between character and reader is not as great, though, as it would be if the term 'historical' as employed here were to conform exactly to Benveniste's definition. In Galdós' *Novelas contemporáneas*, even the background information is narrated in a more conversational *discours*, rather than as an *histoire*, since it is heavily laden with the present and imperfect tenses, often in the first person. This is owing in part to his pervasive use of colloquial speech, a technique which appears related to the stylistic trait which Proust labeled as the 'eternal imperfect' in Flaubert. The atemporal effect which this achieves contributes to a sense of the character's reality because she is not relegated to a past beyond the reader's realm. In addition, this imperfect facilitates the subtlety of transition to the free indirect style.[20] Yet Rosalía is still not as near to the reader in this type of narration as she would be if she were describing herself. The narrator's description labels her and thus makes her more distanced. In this introduction there is no doubt that Rosalía's 'manía nobilaria' is a product of her 'fantasía': 'toda la ciencia heráldica del mundo no justifica que se llamase, con sonoridad rotunda, Rosalía Pipaón de la Barca. Esto lo pronunciaba dando a su bonita y pequeña nariz una hinchazón enfática, rasgo físico que marcaba con infalible precisión lo mismo sus accesos de soberbia que las resoluciones de su bien templada voluntad (IV. 1459–60). Through their common medium of expression, Rosalía's 'hinchazón enfática', her 'resoluciones de bien templada voluntad' become one with her 'accesos de soberbia', which the narrator later terms simply 'orgullete cursi'. Hence this mannerism and the 'sonoridad rotunda' of her speech are examples of the constant allusions to behaviors, gestures, and intonations which mock the self-conception behind them, while effecting an unmistakable humanity and humor.

The initial view of Rosalía is not entirely negative, for she is vigorous – if overbearing – and attractive. The description of her appearance, 'una de esas hermosuras gordas' (IV. 1460), manipulates one of those conventions which draws the reader to the character by implying his familiarity with the type described. Her feeling of superiority and pride in her new home, although rather exaggerated, are not extraordinary. But she is linked to 'la señora de García Grande, su amiga cariñosa' (IV. 1463), the parasitic go-between of El amigo Manso. She, and the other friends of Rosalía already introduced, contribute greatly to the reader's critical view of her and of her social world. Cándida García Grande, Milagros Tellería, José María Manuel del Pez, and others have been ironically presented as minor characters in other novels. Even their names contribute to the irony: Cándida is anything but candid; Milagros miraculously acquires and spends money; and Pez reminds one of the countless administrative types like him who swim in the bureaucratic ocean.[21] All are parasites on society – just as Rosalía is – and this special status is an important element in the irony of her portrayal, in these novels, and in much of Galdós' other work; it is an irony which speaks directly to the reader's world. Rosalía's last words, the last of Tormento, sustain this theme, which is developed further in La de Bringas. Rosalía is furious that Amparo is finally leaving with her fiancé Agustín. She had hoped for a continued parasitic relationship with her relative, and insults Amparo for what she herself was and would gladly have continued to be: 'Sanguijuela de aquel bendito, nos veremos las caras' (IV. 1569). This parasitism, the narrator periodically indicates, is even worse in the society of the 1880s: 'Hoy el parasitismo tiene otro carácter y causas más dañadas y vergonzosas' (IV. 1474).

The narrative becomes more critical of Rosalía as it recounts her relationship with Amparo. Her attitude toward her protégée is correlated with her claims to nobility and with the absurdity of such vainglorious pride in general. Her ridiculous presumption was already revealed: 'Al sacar a relucir su abolengo, no recordaba la señora de Bringas timbres gloriosos de la política o las armas, sino aquellos más bajos, ganados en el servicio inmediato y oscuro de la real persona' (IV. 1459). She despises Amparo (and her sister Refugio) because their side of the family did not enjoy so 'high' a social standing. The narrator remarks that this type of pride was nonetheless typical of society:

La posición social de Rosalía Pipaón de la Barca de Bringas no era, a pesar de su contacto con Palacio y con familias de viso, la más a propósito para fomentar en ella pretensiones aristocráticas de alto vuelo; pero tenía un orgullete cursi, que le inspiraba a menudo, con ahuecamiento de nariz, evocaciones declamatorias de los méritos y calidad de sus antepasados. Gustaba, asimismo...de encarecer sus buenas relaciones. En una sociedad como aquélla, o como ésta, pues la variación de dieciséis años no ha sido muy grande; en esta sociedad, digo, no vigorizada por el trabajo, y en la cual tienen más valor que en otra parte los parentescos, las recomendaciones, los compadrazgos y amistades, la iniciativa individual es sustituída por la fe en las relaciones...En esto de vivir *bien relacionada*, la señora de Bringas no cedía a ningún nacido ni por nacer, y desde tan sólida base se remontaba a la excelsitud de su orgullete español, el cual vicio tiene por fundamento la inveterada pereza del espíritu, la ociosidad de muchas generaciones y la falta de educación intelectual y moral. (IV. 1464–5)

The distance which has enabled the reader to criticize Rosalía so freely is eliminated. If he condemns her actions now, he must also condemn those of his society, and perhaps of himself. Through the satiric portrait of Rosalía, then, the narrator is able to ironize the reader who is caught unawares criticizing his own society and its *orgullete cursi–español*, politics, morals, intellect, and lack of spirit and initiative. The above passage from *Tormento* is not unlike the introduction of *La desheredada*, which compared Leganés to Madrid. In this case, however, Rosalía is made the ironic example from the beginning, while the specific exemplarity of Isidora evolved more indirectly. Rosalía is from the first the object of criticism in *Tormento*, where she epitomizes the restrictive and cruel hypocrisy of her society. She evolves in *La de Bringas*, however, into almost more of a victim than Amparo is in *Tormento*.

In *La de Bringas*, the narrator provides less direct aid to the reader in characterizing Rosalía, employing other more indirect means of portraiture. Because the reader becomes responsible for making more of the judgments regarding Rosalía and her society, his involvement increases and he must make some more frequent re-evaluations of the novel's significance. As the distance between reader and character narrows, so the irony becomes more complex and the satire decreases in severity. In *La de Bringas* no extended history precedes or accompanies the presentation of Rosalía. Although one might suppose that most readers were familiar with both novels, the language in each is so different that they demand consideration as separate ironic discourses. In *La de Bringas* there is an extensive use of the free indirect style, while in *Tormento* it is relegated mostly to the commonplace functions of exclamation and interrogation.[22] The juxtapositions of Rosalía to other characters in *La de Bringas* are more complex and varied than those in *Tormento*, where she is nearly always the adversary. There she becomes almost a stereotype of the wicked stepmother through her cruelty to Amparo and conniving attempt to seduce Agustín. The reader's awareness of this type will determine his reaction to Rosalía's treatment of her children, who are undernourished because the Bringas save money to dress for the theater (IV. 1473–5). Similarly, they withhold the subsistence wages from Amparo; Rosalía pays her instead by 'entregándole con ademán espléndido dos mantecadas de Astorga que, por las muchas hormigas que tenían, creyérase que iban a andar solas' (IV. 1480). As a seductress, Rosalía goes so far as to wish for her husband's death so that she can marry Agustín for his money (IV. 1471). What saves her from becoming a stereotype in *Tormento* and makes her exemplary for the reader is the sense of her plausibility, which is achieved chiefly through the numerous clauses describing her mental and physical idiosyncrasies.

Little is seen of Rosalía in the first few chapters of the highly ironic introduction to *La de Bringas*. The few references to her establish, however, the principal connotative features which constitute her portrait and are particularly outstanding because of their unconventional sentence structure and wording. These features are not historical details, as in *Tormento*; still, they maintain a distance from the reader which is greater than that provided in the initial glimpse of Isidora. In these few lines the major ironic characteristics of Rosalía are foretold: her fatuity, narrow-mindedness, extreme pride, vanity, and obsession with exterior appearances. Little more than a sentence or two is devoted to her in each of the first eight chapters. The first of these, occurring in chapter II, emphasizes her personal shortcomings and her parasitism, and defines the broader ironic movement of the entire novel. Chapter II opens with a discussion of Manuel Pez, the 'próvido sujeto adminis-

trativo' who has arranged for the employment of the Bringas' inept
scion, Paquito:

Sin aguardar a que Paquito se hiciera licenciado en dos o tres Derechos,
habíale adjudicado un empleíllo en Hacienda con cinco mil realetes, lo
que no es mal principio de carrera burocrática a los dieciséis años mal
cumplidos. Toda la sal de este nombramiento, que por lo temprano
parecía el agua del bautismo, estaba en que mi niño, atareado con sus
clases de la Universidad y con aquellas lecturas de Filosofía, de la Historia
y de Derecho de gentes a que se entregaba con furor, no ponía los pies en
la oficina más que para cobrar los cuatrocientos dieciséis reales y pico que
le regalábamos cada mes por su linda cara. (IV. 1574)

The irony of this passage is highlighted by words and phrases such as
'dos o tres Derechos' (when there were, of course, only two: Civil and
Canon), 'realetes', 'reales y pico', 'años mal cumplidos', 'linda cara',
and especially by the subordinate clauses in which the narrator's
clarification confirms the tone: 'lo que no es mal principio', 'que por lo
temprano', 'atareado con sus clases'. The use of the first-person
possessive in 'mi niño' contributes to a sense of deprecatory familiarity.
And the first-person plural 'regalábamos' makes it clear that the reader
is also contributing to this administrative waste, and thus personalizes
his relationship to such a state of affairs.

The next sentence introduces Rosalía by describing her reaction;
because of its ironic tone and juxtaposition to the preceding remarks,
it establishes her complicity in, and profit from, securing this sinecure:
'Aunque en el engreído meollo de Rosalía de Bringas se había incrustado la idea de que la credencial aquella no era favor, sino el
cumplimiento de un deber del Estado para con los españoles precoces,
estaba agradecidísima a la diligencia con que Pez hizo entender y
cumplir a la patria sus obligaciones' (IV. 1574). In this sentence the
author has chosen to invert the standard order of subject followed by
verb. The qualifying clause beginning with 'aunque' precedes the main
part of the sentence 'estaba agradecidísima'. This stylistic inversion of
the sentence is especially functional in creating nuances of meaning.
Ullman has discussed such inversions in the French novel, illustrating
how they serve for emphasis, further irony and parody, and give the
impression of relaying the process of perception. Rosalía's vain reaction
is emphasized in this passage because it precedes her gratitude. The
reader receives the impression that this vanity is indeed her first
response. The thanks that she does express are compromised because
she considers Pez's act as the obligation – not the favor – of a *patria*

which includes the reader. The free indirect style begins with 'la credencial aquella'; its use conveys the narrator's ironic, mocking acquiescence to Rosalía's mode of expression, rather than a sympathetic merger of voices as occurred in Isidora's introduction. The narrator's refusal to directly qualify Rosalía's exaggerated terms, 'cumplimiento', 'deber', 'diligencia', 'cumplir', and the valuation of her insipid son as an 'español precoz', leaves the reader responsible for evaluating her feelings of superiority. Only the inversion of elements in this sentence counteracts the subtlety of Rosalía's ironic introduction and the possible confusion of its narrative voices. This stylistic deviation is the chief indicator, or 'decoder', as Michael Riffaterre terms it,[23] of the deep-seated irony surrounding Rosalía at this point. Since linguistic inversion is 'a literary construction, alien to ordinary speech in all but its simplest forms', it serves as 'an effective means of linguistic portrayal and parody'.[24] Its use here is even more revealing of Rosalía's character since the free indirect style is relaying the sequence of thought rather than of speech.

The sense of 'just dues' intimated in this passage pervades the entire novel. Rosalía listens indulgently to the constant romantic praise which Pez gives her, for example, believing 'que las merecía muy bien, y... que...la sociedad tenía con ella deudas de homenaje...Venía a ser Pez, en buena ley, el desagraviador de ella, el que, en nombre de la sociedad, le pagaba olvidados tributos' (IV. 1618). This passage occurs in the central chapter of the novel, at a point where the duality of her role as exploiter and victim comes to the fore. For Pez, rather than paying society's tribute to her, as she believes, instead personifies its corrupting force. Their adultery illustrates how Rosalía herself becomes a moral and financial victim, while trying to victimize another.

It is noteworthy that the first words referring to Rosalía in the novel associate her intellectual faculties with her pride. The cause of many of her problems is not only a greatly distorted sense of her own importance, but the ignorance which accompanies it. Both concepts are aptly and humorously suggested by the terms 'engreído meollo', while 'se había incrustado' solidifies the image of narrow-mindedness. This is the only reference to Rosalía until the next chapter, where the quality of her intelligence is again under scrutiny. She praises the ridiculous hair-cenotaph Bringas is making in gratitude to the Pez family, an effort which is both the material and symbolic cause of his future physical and moral blindness. (His miserliness prevents him from buying Pez a gift and thereby saving his eyes; his miserliness also makes him blind to Rosalía's needs, and these finally become obsessions in response to Bringas' neglect.) Rosalía's appreciation of Bringas' effort, which, the narrator notes, 'decía la Pipaón con entusiasmo inteligente' (IV. 1576), reflects her inability to see the extreme impracticality of such precise imitations, which she herself will parallel in her dress.

The third reference to Rosalía, in chapter v, alludes to this parallel topic – her fervor for clothing. One room of the Bringas' apartment in the palace 'servía a Rosalía de guardarropa y de cuarto de labor' (IV. 1580); it becomes the locus of her furtive dress-making. The chapter closes with this paragraph: 'En la vecindad había familias a quienes Rosalía, con todo su orgullete, no tenía más remedio que conceptuar superiores. Otras estaban muy por bajo de su grandeza pipaónica; pero con todas se trataba y a todas devolvió la ceremoniosa visita inaugural de su residencia en la población superpalatina. Doña Cándida...' (IV. 1581). Again her mental processes are referred to with the verb 'conceptuar' which is associated with her pride by the prepositional phrase 'con todo su orgullete'. The narrator parodies her by entitling her – as she herself might – 'su grandeza pipaónica'. Throughout the novel – as well as in *Tormento, La desheredada,* and others where the protagonists' portraits are radically ironic – Rosalía's self-concept is used to parody her presumption with frequent plays on her name. The idea of a 'visita inaugural' indentifies the Bringas with the royal family; both live beyond their means, bringing about revolution. The concluding mention of Cándida in this paragraph, like her recurrence throughout the novel, indicates that the parasitic connotations surrounding Rosalía and the palace will not disappear for a moment. In the following chapter (VI) the narrator refreshes the reader's memory of Cándida, indirectly reminding him of her role as a go-between in *El amigo Manso*. Rosalía's affection for her is then described: 'Rosalía sentía hacia ella respetuoso afecto y la oía siempre con sumisión, conceptuándola como gran autoridad en materias sociales y en toda suerte de elegancias... Esta aureola fascinaba a Rosalía, quien, extremando su respeto a las majestades caídas, aparentaba tomar en serio aquello de *mi administrador*' (IV. 1582). The information which the narrator subsequently provides concerning Doña Cándida assures that the reader will recognize Rosalía's inability to judge character. The relationship of Rosalía to Cándida shows the extent of her cult of that exteriority in which Cándida, like Milagros and Pez, excels, rather than any appreciation – or even perception – of interior value. Rosalía is attracted by any appearance of splendor and elegance, no matter how slight. The sequence of words in the passage quoted above marks her relationship with luxury: 'sumisión...conceptuándola...autoridad...elegancia...fascinaba...aparentaba'. She even strives to be elegant through her children: 'La juguetona bandada de mujeres a medio formar invadía el domicilio de Bringas. Rosalía, gozosa de tratarse con doña Tula, con los Tellerías, con los Lantiguas, recibíalas con los brazos abiertos, y las obsequiaba con dulces, que se hacía traer previamente de la repostería de Palacio' (IV. 1584). The descriptive clause, 'gozosa de tratarse con doña Tula' undermines her intention, leaving no doubt that she does not invite the children to play out of love for them, nor out of generosity, as the clause identifying the source of the 'dulces' indicates. Although she is portrayed as a concerned mother in *La de Bringas*, this attribute is continually compromised by her vanity. After buying some 'cosillas' for the children in one instance, the narrator comments that 'no gustaba de componerse ella sola, sino que tenía vanidad de emperejilar bien a sus hijos para que alternaran dignamente con los niños de otras familias' (IV. 1591). As with Isidora, any positive characteristic Rosalía might exhibit is eventually belied by a compromising behavior.

The highly satiric 'feeding of the poor' in chapter VII becomes a show for the elegant ladies of the palace and symbolizes the hypocrisy of the monarchy's official charity. Here Rosalía is in her element: 'Rosalía también se personó en la regla morada, juzgando que era indispensable su presencia para que las ceremonias tuviesen todo el brillo y pompa convenientes' (IV. 1584). Although the narrator subsequently describes the 'farsa de aquel cuadro teatral' (IV. 1585) in mordantly satiric detail, the reader confronted here with Rosalía's vain musings may recognize that it is his own society which has deemed such pomp and splendor appropriate to the simple and unaffected exercise of Christian charity. Rosalía is a highly incriminating spokesman for her society's values, because her judgments of propriety and etiquette regularly lack any foundation in reality. In the culminating scene in which she condescends to borrow money from Refugio, she still maintains an attitude of superiority to the orphan: 'La Pipaón pensó así:...¿qué más honra quieres que prestar tu dinero a una persona como yo?' (IV. 1661). Besides the notion that anyone is honored who lends her money, her idea of 'una persona como yo' is ironic. For the reader knows that Rosalía is little better than Refugio at this point in the novel, having committed the same adulterous act for which she continually condemns her and her sister Amparo.

The initial ironic allusions to Rosalía in *La de Bringas* epitomize the construction of her portrait and of the novel as a whole. Their stylized language serves to produce the often oblique irony of her description. The semes of vanity, presumption, and ignorance which traverse her portrait reflect on her society and provide the reader with an indirect comment on his own world. Just as he must penetrate the stylized language of the novel in order to perceive its irony, so he must penetrate the conventions of his own society in order to perceive its farce. Yet Rosalía is not simply a stylized *cursi* to be typed and thus rendered parodic; the non-stereotypical elements of her character make its irony all the more applicable to the reader himself. Although Rosalía is not as sympathetic a figure as Isidora, she is not nearly so one-sided as in *Tormento*. Often motivated by pride in her children, Rosalía's love for them is sincere. She also tries to be a good wife to her avaricious older husband and is truely pained by his blindness. She even loses the desire for elegant clothing during the first part of his illness. Rosalía often criticizes Bringas' selfishness, but quickly adds, for example, that 'era muy bueno, eso sí, esposo sin pero y padre excelente'. But 'no sabía colocar a su mujer en el rango que por su posición correspondía a entrambos' (IV. 1600). The alternation between her desire to be a good wife and her craving for elegance continues in spite of his extreme miserliness. But when she discovers from his hoarded savings the true degree of his avarice, her subsequent descriptions reflect a permanent change in her attitude: '¡Oh, qué hombre tan ñoño!' (IV. 1632). Rosalía belies her haughty self-concept by the use of a purely proletarian expression. The change in her codes of expression and ideation corresponds to a change in the code of social values which she acknowledges. She abandons both the vocabulary and behavior of penurious practicality and uncompromising morality in order to assume those of prodigal impracticality and (soon) duplicitous immorality: 'El descubrimiento del tesoro sacó las ideas de Rosalía de aquel círculo de modestia y abnegación en que las había encerrado la enfermedad de su marido' (IV. 1632). Having lived so long in submission to one extreme code of superficial and hypocritical values, behavior, and expression, Rosalía is unable to temper her compliance with another equally extreme, superficial, and hypocritical code.

The complex of interwoven codes in *La de Bringas* makes the analysis of its language especially interesting. As in *La desheredada* the narrative levels of character, plot, and theme are essentially ironic reflections of each other. But this specularity is intensified in its focus on the problem of mimesis, or realism; the novel is an acutely self-reflective commentary. The introductory hair-cenotaph (which will be discussed in detail in chapter 2 of this study) is an ironic statement about mimetic art explicitly and about the novel implicitly. It is also a comment on Rosalía's obsessive imitation of the fashions of the queen and the figures surrounding her. The overthrow of Isabel II is imminent because she is unable to deal with the real problems of her government; Rosalía is unable to deal with the reality of her social and economic position. The facts that the Bringas family lives in the Palacio Nacional, and that Bringas also becomes a useless consort, reinforce this parallel. The decay of Rosalía's moral character in the novel seems to reflect that of Spain in her day, particularly that of the middle and upper classes, who ignore the limits of their circumstances in order to imitate the profligacy of the higher classes. Rosalía imitates the excesses of Milagros Tellería, who imitates those of the queen. But this structure of reflection is not a series of faithful images, rather counterfeit ones, just as verisimilitude is a simulation, a counterfeit of reality.

Rosalía's emancipation from Bringas and his code of morality also makes her a parallel to the revolutionaries. But at the same time as Rosalía learns to deal effectively with her society through revolution, that very society is ironically exposed as superficial. Her reality, then, as she becomes adept at a type of highly paid prostitution, is one of parasitism and appearance; her life reflects the novelistic society around her, and, we are told, the reader's own. Golfín, Bringas' eye-doctor, is ironically unable to see the penurious condition behind their appearance of luxury. Even an eye-doctor is unable to see clearly. The narrator explains that 'aquel Golfín era un poco inocente en cosas del mundo, y... conocía mal nuestras costumbres y esta especialidad del vivir madrileño' (IV. 1634): these special customs included living and appearing beyond one's means. It is not just Rosalía's life-style, but that of all Madrid, both before and after the revolution.

The ironic parallel between Rosalía and the Revolution of 1868 is especially obvious at the end of the novel where the novelistic and the historical worlds seem to coincide. Double meanings are intensified, as in this instance: 'La revolución era cosa mala, según decían todos; pero tambíen era lo desconocido, y lo desconocido atrae las imaginaciones exaltadas, y seduce a los que se han creado en su vida una situación irregular. Vendrían otros tiempos, otro modo de ser, algo nuevo, estupendo y que diera juego. "En fin —pensaba ella—, veremos eso."'

(IV. 1667). The 'imaginación exaltada' and 'situación irregular' apply directly to Rosalía. The use of the verb 'seducir' is intensely ironic in view of her adulterous enterprises. The ambiguity of the passage is furthered because it is unclear whether the 'algo nuevo, estupendo y que diera juego' is hers or the narrator's. The final paragraphs of the novel complete this ironic interplay of political and moral codes: Rosalía, 'un tanto majestuosa', takes over her 'papel de piedra angular de la casa' 'en plena época revolucionaria'. Her appearance may be majestic, but her firm foundation is that of prostitution and parasitism. She creates a 'ruinosa amistad' with everyone she meets. The ultimate irony is that she is offered as a symbol of both the monarchy and the revolution, and thus embraces the political spectrum of the reader's society.

The extent to which the portrait of Rosalía becomes an ironic commentary on many aspects of political and historical Spain, as well as a sort of 'irony of manners', is apparent in these last paragraphs of *La de Bringas*. The image of her as 'majestuosa', like many other allusions already noted, make her a parallel to Isabel II; the condemnation of Rosalía's moral and economic values thus becomes one of Queen Isabel. But the behavior she learned under the monarchy is to be perfected under the Republic:

Las nuevas trazas de esta señora no están aún en nuestro tintero. Lo que sí puede asegurarse, por referencias bien comprobadas, es que en lo sucesivo supo la de Bringas triunfar fácilmente y con cierto donaire de las situaciones penosas que le creaban sus irregularidades...no tuvo que afanarse tanto como en ocasiones parecidas, descritas en este libro. Y es que tales ocasiones, lances, dramas mansos, o como quiera llamárselos, fueron los ensayos de aquella mudanza moral, y debieron de cogerla inexperta y como novicia. (IV. 1670)

The adventures of Rosalía's pre-revolutionary 'novitiate' prepared her to lead a more perfect, but hardly monastic, life after the events of 1868. These ironic references to her later triumphs imply a correspondingly ironic view of post-Isabelline morality and politics, including, perhaps, the reader's own era. In other passages Rosalía's actions are associated more with liberal and progressive programs than with traditional and conservative ones. During one of her nights of insomnia, she recalls her miserable honeymoon and subsequent years of financial and emotional penury with Bringas. The passage is presented in the free indirect style and in an apparently sympathetic tone. Near the end of her account she expresses a modest desire for a little freedom in her life: 'para sí anhelaba ardientemente algo más que vida y salud: deseaba un poco, un poquito siquiera de lo que nunca había tenido, libertad, y salir, aunque sólo fuera por modo figurado, de aquella estrechez vergonzante. Porque, lo decía con sinceridad, envidiaba a los mendigos, pues éstos, el ochavo que tienen lo gozan con libertad, mientras que ella...' (IV. 1627). As always, when some aspect of Rosalía is treated sympathetically, it ultimately becomes ironic. Here the final twist is quite subtle; Rosalía's concept of 'libertad', a term which connotes grand and humane ideals, is purely materialistic and personal. It is a comment, perhaps, on Spanish liberals.

La de Bringas is a more consistently ironic text than, for example, La desheredada. This is partly so because it does not develop any elaborate intrigue or dramatic suspense. The time span of La de Bringas is almost totally limited to the months preceding September 1868 and the locus of activity is confined to the Bringas' apartment in the palace. The protagonist's preoccupations, while in many ways similar to Isidora's, appear more shallow because there are no 'extenuating circumstances'; Rosalía does not believe she is the disinherited heiress to a marquesado, and all her activity is directed toward acquiring, paying for, and going into debt for clothing. Such a concerted pursuit of superficial appearance is an easy subject for irony and satire. The novel is much shorter than La desheredada, so there is less need for 'historical' narrative and more opportunity for ironic discourse. Linguistic devices which serve irony are employed more frequently and make the narrative more complex. The use of theatricalized dialogue when Rosalía discusses her dresses, the numerous interior monologues, and the frequent use of the free indirect style all diversify the portrait of Rosalía by allowing the reader to see many sides of her personality from varying distances. The alternation of narrative voices is highly sophisticated in La de Bringas, and they are usually combined with great subtlety. At the beginning of chapter XI, for example, Rosalía tells her husband one of many lies about the source of her new clothes:

Se determinó, sí, y para explicar la posesión de tan soberbia gala, tuvo que apelar al recursillo, un tanto gastado ya, de la munificencia de su majestad. Aquí de las casualidades. Hallándose Rosalía en la Cámara Real en el momento que destapaban unas cajas recién llegadas de París, la reina se probó un canesú que le venía estrecho...Luego, de una caja preciosa...una tela que parecía rasete...sacaron tres manteletas. Una de ellas le caía maravillosamente a su majestad; las otras dos, no. 'Ponte ésa, Rosaliíta...Ni pintada.' En efecto...Faltó poco para que a mi buen Thiers se le saltaran las lágrimas oyendo el bien contado relato.

Si no estoy equivocado, la deglución de esta gran bola por el ancho tragadero de don Francisco acaeció en abril. (IV. 1590)

This narration which occurs in the novelistic past ('abril'), is related in such a skillful free indirect style that it almost seems to be taking place at the moment of reading. Rosalía's 'fiction' becomes almost visible in such passages where she herself seems to become both narrator and author. This skillful merger enhances the subtlety of the text, and contributes to the reader's possible confusion. This ambiguous alternation of voices is frequent, as in the following passage:

La boca de Rosalía tenía un sello. No osaba pronunciar una sola palabra...Confesar a su marido el aprieto en que se veía era declarar una serie de atentados clandestinos contra la economía doméstica, que era la segunda religión de Bringas. Pero si Dios no le deparaba una solución, érale forzoso apechugar con aquel doloroso remedio...No, Cristo Padre; era preciso inventar algo, buscar, revolver medio mundo...Antes que vender al economista el secreto de sus compras...optaba por hacer el sacrificio de sus galas, por arrancarse aquellos pedazos de su corazón que se manifestaban en mundo real en forma de telas, encajes y cintas. (IV. 1607)

The transition from narrative description to a free indirect method of communicating Rosalía's thoughts occurs somewhere between the sentences beginning with 'Confesar' and 'No, Cristo'. The belief that God would provide a solution to her indebtedness is clearly ironic, yet the sheer conventionality of such a notion might facilitate its irony passing unnoticed by the reader.

More common uses of the free indirect style frequently occur in exclamation and interrogation. As Rosalía contemplates how to conceal her expenditures from Bringas, her voice takes over and poses a question: 'Rosalía se desvelaba pensando en los embustes que habían de servirle de descargo en caso de sorpresa. ¿Con qué patrañas explicaría el crecimiento grande de la riqueza y variedad de su guardarropa?' (IV. 1598). The humorous term 'patrañas' is obviously hers, and the subsequent description of her fear continues in the free indirect style. Sometimes an exclamation or interrogation is combined with statements whose speaking subject is not clear. At the beginning of chapter XXI Bringas goes blind, causing Rosalía both to grieve for his catastrophe and feel joy for the solution it offers to her debts: 'Pero casi al mismo tiempo que tal decía vínole rápidamente al pensamiento, como esos rayos celestes de que nos habla el misticismo, una idea salvadora, una solución fácil, eficacísima, derivada, ¡oh rarezas de la vida!, de la misma situación aflictiva en que la familia se encontraba. ¡Qué cosas hace Dios! Él sabrá por qué las hace' (IV. 1610). The exclamations are Rosalía's but the concept of 'una idea salvadora' may be ambiguous. Again, if the reader agrees with the possibility of divine intervention in such a mundane affair, he accepts the commonplace which is ironized.

These religious references in the narration constitute another code which becomes ironic as it traverses Rosalía's portrait. She continually sees 'los cielos abiertos', as, for example, when she obtains a loan from Torres (IV. 1644), or when she hears of Pez's imminent return (IV. 1655). This instance is doubly ironic since she plans to obtain money from him through adultery. She even asks God to bring Pez soon, so she can sell herself: 'Rosalía se conceptuaba dichosa al ver delante de sí aquellos días de respiro. En este tiempo vendría Pez quizá. Trajérale Dios pronto' (IV. 1654). Her uncritical self-concept is recalled in 'se conceptuaba'. This passage is juxtaposed to Rosalía's thoughts about Refugio, whom she judges to be immoral. She tells herself that she would rather prostitute herself than ask a prostitute (Refugio) for money, which she must eventually do anyway. Yet her condemnation of Refugio softens when she hears that she has become a *modista*: 'la de Bringas oíala con algún interés, perdonando quizá el vilipendio de la persona por la excelsitud del asunto que trataba. Así como el Espíritu Santo, bajando a los labios del pecador arrepentido, puede sanctificar a éste, Refugio, a los ojos de su ilustre pariente, se redimía por la divinidad de su discurso' (IV. 1622). This parody of Rosalía's ideas and of her self-concept as 'ilustre' is especially humorous because of their superficiality. The association of 'divinity' and 'seamstress' parodies Rosalía's approach to both by grossly vulgarizing the first and exaggerating the importance of the second; that Refugio could be sanctified in becoming a *modista* suggests the primacy which clothing has attained in Rosalía's system of values, while underscoring the banality of her religiosity. Throughout the novel the terms with which she describes and reacts to fashion illustrate the great discrepancy between the value of the object and her appreciation of it. Her obsession is labeled 'pasión de vestir' and she esteems Milagros for her 'exquisito gusto en materia de trapos y modas'. Her reaction to even the thought of dresses is extraordinary. In the 'stage directions' of the theatrical dialogue with Milagros the narrator explains that the scene is offered in this way so that 'el exótico idioma de los trapos no pierda su genialidad castiza' (IV. 1588). He then describes Rosalía 'contemplando en éxtasis lo que aún no es más que una abstracción', with 'ansioso interés', and 'embebecida'. This passion, the narrator indicates, causes her fall from paradise: 'me la echó de aquel Paraíso en que su Bringas la tenía tan sujeta' (IV. 1588). Yet the narrative invocations of paradise and original sin (especially in chapter IX) are themselves ironic reflections of the method used to parody Rosalía's passions and expression. The narrator, too, uses exalted terms for a trivial subject. The subtle parody of Rosalía's style of expression by the narrator is another example of the novel's replete specularity. The novel not only represents Rosalía and the manners of her society to the reader for his ironic evaluation, but constitutes an ironic comment on its own pretense to representation.

The hyperbolic and often catachrestic language of Rosalía's obsessions establishes the irony of her imitated values: terms such as 'exótico idioma', 'éxtasis', 'exquisito gusto', etc., contrast violently with 'trapos'. These kinds of linguistic oppositions pervade the novel; they constitute the minimum level of a structure of conciliated opposition which composes the irony of the portrait as a whole. References to her mental processes are especially incongruous: 'La ingeniosa dama no hallaba blanduras semejantes, sino algo duro y con picos que le tenía en desasosiego toda la noche. Porque su pasión de lujo la había llevado, insensiblemente, a un terreno erizado de peligros' (IV. 1597). The term 'ingeniosa' is frequently used when Rosalía is lying or posturing with Bringas, along with references to her 'imaginación' and 'entendimiento'; these are juxtaposed to terms suggesting unawareness, ignorance, and stupidity, just as 'ingeniosa' and 'insensiblemente' in the passage above. Such terms call Don Quijote to mind, with its corresponding irony of the disparity between imagination or perception, and the world. Terms describing her role and the comedy she performs reinforce this conflict of the real and the unreal and suggest the dual irony of her fiction within the novel's fiction (a concept which is itself a fiction, of course).[25]

The oppositions which Rosalía – like Isidora before her – perceives are the inverse of those the reader sees. Rosalía's belief in her superiority over Refugio and Amparo is entirely her own. Her social origin is no better than theirs, nor is she more 'moral'. Rosalía's agony in the final scene with Refugio is dramatically and verbally ironic in many ways.[26] Rosalía asks for money from one who was supposedly under her protection, but whom she only abused; Refugio on the other hand does help Rosalía in turn. Refugio's ironic 'por usted o por don Francisco haría los imposibles, y me quitaría el pan de la boca' (IV. 1661), is in fact what she and her sister Amparo did. They did far more work for the Bringas than was required, without receiving sufficient money or food for existence. Refugio's subtle insults are in fact truthful and seemingly well-deserved, especially to the reader of *Tormento*. However, the narrator does not let his audience escape untouched by this scene of Rosalía's humiliation, whose crowning blow is the shock of learning that Milagros Tellería considers her *cursi*. As she looks in the mirror afterwards to see if she has any gray hairs, he remarks: 'Digámoslo para tranquilidad de las damas que en situación semejante se pudieran ver. No le había salido ninguna cana. Y si le salieron, no se le conocían. Y si se le conocieran, ya habría ella buscado el medio de taparlas' (IV. 1666). Rosalía's hypocrisy, which includes the reader through the first-person plural as well as through the parenthetical remark addressed to 'las damas', is reflected in the linguistic structure of this passage. Each sentence advances a step further her hypocritical process of covering reality with appearances.

Rosalía's relationships with other characters are not as complicated as those with Refugio, for her various associates are more like her, dedicated to creating reality out of appearance. Milagros, Pez, and other minor social figures who appear – as well as some of those who do not (such as Isabel II and Madrid society) – are just as oriented to exterior appearances as Rosalía. Her actions belie her apparent penetration of Milagros' superficiality. In chapter XIV Rosalía describes her critically to Bringas, telling him of her friend's problems with money and her husband. Rosalía is in fact describing herself here, even when hinting at a justification for Milagros' love affairs. Rosalía suggests that she is 'muy gastadora' (IV. 1596), since money just slips through her fingers – '*adiós mi dinero*'. Besides the self-description, there is a situational irony here: Rosalía has just lent Milagros the money that she herself borrowed elsewhere. The *frase hecha* calls attention to the irony of its literal meaning. She comes to understand the shallowness of Pez only too late, after being attracted to him by his appearance and his employment: 'Si Pez no hubiera sido empleado, habría perdido mucho a sus ojos, acostumbrados a ver el mundo como si todo él fuera una oficina y no se conocieran otros medios de vivir que los del presupuesto. Luego aquel aire elegante, aquella levita negra cerrada' (IV. 1618). Rosalía is rudely awakened and infuriated to 'venderse y no cobrar nuestro precio' (IV. 1657). Only then does she come to terms with the consequences of superficiality.

The ironically specular relationships between the characters of *La de Bringas* reflect others which constitute the individual portrait of Rosalía, and the novel as a whole. In so far as the novel pretends to reflect society at large, the reader must constantly attend to the possible extra-textual import of this specularity. His attention is especially necessary when these ironic relationships redirect or readjust the images and reflections which the characters themselves or their society have affirmed. The novel presents a society whose fictions frequently prohibit it from seeing its own image clearly. In Rosalía's perspective, her fictions are her reality; in the novel each character's values are systematically undermined, whether he realizes it or not. The reader may strive to evaluate Rosalía, the novel, and his own society with the distance of an ultimate objectivity, but his evaluation, too, is only relative. This was the lesson which Don Quijote and his reader learned, and which Galdós has taught once more through the ironic language of his novels.

Galdós' creation of portrait is an integral component of his ironic art. The character is composed of literary and cultural codes with which the reader is familiar. Frequently this conventional knowledge is ironically reversed so that the information with which the reader makes the portrait intelligible must be re-evaluated. The reader's own values will inevitably be affected by the critical imperative which results from such an ironic vision. Through character, the primary focus of many nineteenth-century novels, a structure of reflection can be observed which informs the entire text and extends to the act of reading itself. The ironic distortion of this structure is itself only an instance of that irony which pervades all realities and makes all perceptions – all readings – ultimately only subjective, never absolutely objective.

The setting of irony

The introductory scenes of Galdós' novels invariably foreshadow the ironic themes of the entire work, while at the same time epitomizing the structure of those ironies. These descriptions of settings present the multiple meanings which the reader will encounter: the apparent (literal) and the deeper (figurative) levels of *vraisemblance*. When these levels come into contradiction, their significance changes from the metaphorical to the ironic. The scenes described no longer remain straightforward statements, but become ironic commentaries upon the codes of meaning traversing the text, as well as on themselves, and thus become intrinsically self-ironizing. The reader is responsible for seeing beyond the first, apparent meaning by recognizing stylistic clues in the language. The ironic significance of the setting described, like that of the portrait, is understood through, while being reflected in, its linguistic composition. This specular relationship between 'meaning' and 'form' parallels, in turn, the homology between the reader's comprehension and the stylistic features of the text. Devices such as oxymoron, hyperbole, simile, metaphor, catachresis, inversion, antithesis, anaphora, allegory, and isocolon create and signal the ironic relationships which exist between the several meanings. The frequent combination of styles, from the elaborately literary to the plainly colloquial, ironically contrasts these codes of speech and their corresponding connotations, just as the play of voices in the portrait does. The impressionistic effects which often result illustrate both the variety of ways in which the 'real' might be visualized, and how the ironic significance of the picture is gradually perceived. This is the same process of understanding – or naturalizing – irony at work in the novel as a whole, and in the reader's final evaluation of its importance for him.

The four passages studied here are the introductory settings of *La de Bringas* (1884), *Torquemada y San Pedro* (1895), *Nazarín* (1895), and *Misericordia* (1897). As with the opening scene in Leganés from *La desheredada*, the introduction to a novel frequently sets forth the complex of ironies which develops through the characters, plot, and themes. It is generally in the introductory settings that the presence of the ironic codes is most intense; however, this does not exclude other passages within the novel from displaying considerable ironic tension also. The description of the labyrinthine palace in *La de Bringas*, for example, bears as much ironic symbolism as the introductory hair-cenotaph. Torquemada's return to his old *barrio*, Nazarín's wanderings in the countryside, and Benina's bustling activity among the squalid areas of Madrid all involve settings whose descriptions are intensely ironic in numerous ways. Other novels also offer settings which are memorable for their ironies: *Doña Perfecta*'s Orbajosa, the stormy landscape in *Gloria*, Eloísa's house in *Lo prohibido*, the convent of Las Micaelas in *Fortunata y Jacinta*, and Ángel Guerra's projected religious edifice are just a few examples. The passages cited here are outstanding for their intensification of the ironies present at all levels of Galdós' novels.

La de Bringas

Era aquello... ¿cómo lo diré yo?... un gallardo artificio sepulcral de atrevidísima arquitectura, grandioso de traza, en ornamentos rico, por una parte severo y rectilíneo a la manera viñolesca, por otra movido, ondulante y quebradizo, a la usanza gótica, con ciertos atisbos platerescos donde menos se pensaba, y, por fin, cresterías semejantes a las del estilo tirolés que prevalece en los quioscos. Tenía piramidal escalinata, zócalos grecorromanos, y luego machones y paramentos ojivales, con pináculos, gárgolas y doseletes. Por arriba y por abajo, a izquierda y derecha, cantidad de antorchas, urnas, murciélagos, ánforas, buhos, coronas de siemprevivas, aladas clepsidras, guadañas, palmas, anguilas enroscadas y otros emblemas del morir y del vivir eterno. Estos objetos se encaramaban unos sobre otros, cual si se disputasen, pulgada a pulgada, el sitio que habían de ocupar. En el centro del mausoleo, un angelón de buen talle y mejores carnes se inclinaba sobre una lápida, en actitud atribulada y luctuosa, tapándose los ojos con la mano como avergonzado de llorar, de cuya vergüenza se podía colegir que era varón. Tenía este caballerito ala y media de rizadas y finísimas plumas, que le caían por la trasera con desmayada gentileza, y calzaba sus pies de mujer con botitos, coturnos o alpargatas; que de todo había un poco en aquella elegantísima interpretación de la zapatería angelical. Por la cabeza le corría una como guirnalda con cintas, que se enredaban después en su brazo derecho. Si a primera vista se podía sospechar que el tal gimoteaba por la molestia de llevar tanta cosa sobre sí: alas, flores, cintajos y plumas, amén de un relojito de arena, bien pronto se caía en la cuenta de que el motivo del duelo era la triste memoria de las virginales criaturas encerradas dentro del sarcófago. Publicaban desconsoladamente sus nombres diversas letras compungidas, de cuyos trazos inferiores salían unos lagrimones que figuraban resbalar por el mármol al modo de babas escurridizas. Por tal modo de expresión, las afligidas letras contribuían al melancólico efecto del monumento.

Pero lo más bonito era quizá el sauce, ese arbolito sentimental que de antiguo nombran *llorón*, y que desde la llegada de la Retórica al mundo viene teniendo una participación más o menos criminal en toda elegía que se comete. Su ondulado tronco elevábase junto al cenotafio, y de las altas esparcidas ramas caía la lluvia de hojitas tenues, desmayadas, agonizantes. Daban ganas de hacerle oler algún fuerte alcaloide para que se despabilase y volviera en sí de un poético síncope. El tal sauce era irreemplazable en una época en que aún no se hacía leña de los árboles del romanticismo. El suelo estaba sembrado de graciosas plantas y flores, que se erguían sobre tallos de diversos tamaños. Había margaritas, pensamientos, pasionarias, girasoles, lirios y tulipanes enormes, todos respetuosamente inclinados en señal de tristeza... El fondo o perspectiva consistía en el progresivo alejamiento de otros sauces de menos talla que se iban a llorar a moco y baba camino del horizonte. Más allá veíanse suaves contornos de montañas que ondulaban cayéndose como si estuvieran bebidas; luego había un poco de mar, otro poco de río, el confuso perfil de una ciudad con góticas torres y almenas; y arriba, en el espacio destinado al cielo, una oblea que debía de ser la Luna, a juzgar por los blancos reflejos de ella que esmaltaban las aguas y los montes.

El color de esta bella obra de arte era castaño, negro y rubio. La gradación del oscuro al claro servía para producir ilusiones de perspectiva aérea... Reparad en lo nimio, escrupuloso y firme de tan difícil trabajo. Las hojas del sauce se podrían contar una por una. El artista había querido expresar el conjunto, no por el conjunto mismo, sino por la suma de pormenores, copiando indoctamente a la Naturaleza, y para obtener el follaje tuvo la santa calma de calzarse las hojitas todas una después de otra. Habíalas tan diminutas, que no se podían ver sino con microscopio. Todo el claroscuro del sepulcro consistía en menudos órdenes de bien agrupadas líneas, formando peine y enrejados más o menos ligeros, según la diferente intensidad de los valores. En el modelado del angelote había tintas tan delicadas, que sólo se formaban de una nebulosa de puntos pequeñísimos. Parecía que había caído arenilla sobre el fondo blando. Los tales puntos, imitando el estilo de la talla dulce, se espesaban en los oscuros, se rarificaban y desvanecían en los claros, dando de sí, con esta alterna y bien distribuída masa, la ilusión del relieve... Era, en fin, el tal cenotafio un trabajo de pelo o en pelo, género de arte que tuvo cierta boga, y su autor, don Francisco Bringas, demostraba en él habilidad benedictina, una limpieza de manos y una seguridad de vista que rayaban en lo maravilloso, si no un poquito más allá. (IV. 1573–4)

The first sentence from chapter 1 of *La de Bringas* announces the irony of the passage, just as the entire chapter, an exercise in parodic ekphrasis, announces the irony of the novel as a whole. The structures of the sentence are systematically inverted, reflecting the inverted values of the 'artist' Bringas, his wife Rosalía, and their society, which is a metaphor – or even hyperbole – of Madrid. The sentence calls attention to this inversion; through its pauses it ironizes the object described and its own description by pretending concentrated contemplation. The 'atrevidísima arquitectura' of the object is also that of the language which describes it, replete with hyperbole, and crescendoing to an anticlimax in the inverted syntax and exaggerated vocabulary of the final sentence.[1] This second figuration of the '*objet d'art*' ironically reverses the first through its mirrored syntax, but different valuation. The last sentence, like the first, begins with the prenominal 'Era' and hesitates with 'en fin' before disclosing the subject. But the 'gallardo artificio' has become merely 'el tal cenotafio'. The precise architectural terms have descended to 'trabajo de pelo o en pelo'. The 'estilo tirolés' becomes only another mark of its obsolescence: 'género de arte que tuvo cierta boga'. The preterite here defines not only the obsolescence of the cenotaph, but also the implicit redundancy of its intensely mimetic pretense – which in the narration itself establishes the text's self-parody, as does the final 'si no un poquito más allá'. Bringas' 'maravilloso' imitative ability is ironic at the level of its redundance, and also alludes to the distance from reality of his endeavor, of his pretensions, of the language which describes them, and finally of the novel.

This structure of ironic crescendo occurs throughout the chapter as well as in individual sentences; moreover, it describes Rosalía's banal passions, the political events leading to the Revolution of 1868 as portrayed in the novel, and even the short-lived Revolution itself. An 'angelón de buen talle y mejores carnes' occupies the center of the elaborate elegy; the use of the augmentative and the colloquial physical description emphasize the incongruity of the figure, as do the references to the angel as 'este caballerito' and 'angelote'. The somewhat androgynous description of the angel reflects the conventions of religious art. Only his manner of hiding his tears ('de cuya vergüenza se podía colegir que era varón') belies his otherwise indeterminate gender. This feature of the cenotaph perhaps suggests parodically the sexually repressive aspects of nineteenth-century sentimental piety. The angel's 'pies de mujer' are shod with 'botitos, coturnos, o alpargatas', an economical combination of a plethora of linguistic and social connotations. 'Botitos' is a familiar colloquial term; 'coturnos' invokes a very *culto* image of Classical dress; while 'alpargatas' is evocative of a very popular, if not ignoble, apparel. 'Botitos' contrasts with 'aquella elegantísima interpretación de zapatería angelical'. The phrase 'zapatería angelical' itself combines absurdly incongruous connotations. The inversion employed for archaic and literary effects now sounds simply colloquial, and achieves a notably anticlimactic crescendo in such expressions as 'amén de un relojito de arena' and 'bien pronto se caía en la cuenta'. These expressions contrast again with the succeeding 'triste memoria de las virginales criaturas'. The 'diversas letras cumpungidas' shed 'lagrimones' which become the earthy phrase, 'babas escurridizas'. The conversational 'daban ganas' is stylistically incongruent with the learned 'poético síncope'; the extended hyperbolic description of the 'sauces' colloquially adds that they look as if 'se iban a llorar a moco y baba'. These descriptions exemplify another ironic device used in this scene; it is filled with personifying verbs and adjectives, similes and metaphors. The 'letras' are 'cumpungidas' and 'afligidas', the trees incline 'respetuosamente en señal de tristeza' and the mountains seem 'bebidas'. This vacillation in tone between the highly literary and the colloquial, or the elegant and the ridiculous, combined with the personifications, produces that distortion which the juxtaposition of pompous detail to the directness of colloquial expression achieves. Through such exaggerated linguistic play the ironic and incisive meanings of the narrative become apparent.

'La gradación del oscuro al claro' which the narrator observes in the hair-cenotaph in the last paragraph is indeed the effect of the narration itself as it moves from first sentence to last, from clause to clause, and from word to word. But contrary to Bringas' intention, the 'oscuro' is the exaggerated detail and the 'claro' is its colloquial interpretation by the distanced narrator. The reader may be confused about the 'gallardo artificio' until he is told it is only 'el tal cenotafio...de pelo'. Rosalía simulates the elegant appearance of the socially prominent Tellerías in every superficial detail; she is misled until she realizes – and then accepts – the irony in the fundamental vulgarity of their venal parasitism. Language, too, becomes an illusory façade if one believes it represents exact reality. The first chapter of *La de Bringas*, like the rest of the novel and Galdós' work over all, illustrates how his concept of the novel as an 'imagen de la vida' is no more than an image or metaphor. Language – the novel – is only a metaphor for reality, not reality itself. As such it is intrinsically ironic because metaphor implies an equation of the figurative and the literal, which are forever different.

A hair cenotaph can never be a mausoleum, nor can the novel be reality. Just like Bringas, we become victims of irony if we think otherwise. This passage is a comment on representation, on the novel, and on art in general. Bringas seeks to 'expresar el conjunto, no por el conjunto mismo, sino por la suma de sus pormenores, copiando indoctamente a la Naturaleza' – a sort of reversal of impressionism. The obvious parody of this 'art' and of the 'santa calma' which Bringas achieves through microscopic imitation clearly identifies what the novel is not. *La de Bringas*, like the *Novelas contemporáneas* as a whole, is not a faithful imitation of society, but rather a linguistic construct whose significative relationships are never uniform.

Torquemada y San Pedro

Las primeras claridades de un amanecer lento y pitañoso, como de enero, colándose por claraboyas y tragaluces en el interior del que fué palacio de Gravelinas, iba despertando todas las cosas del sueño de la oscuridad, sacándolas, como quien dice, de la nada negra a la vida pictórica...En la armería, la luz matinal puso el primer toque de color en el plumaje de yelmos y morriones; modeló después con trazo firme los petos y espaldares, los brazales y coseletes, hasta encajar por entero las gallardísimas figuras, en quien no es difícil ver catadura de seres vivos, porque la costra de bruñido hierro cuerpo es de persona monstruosa y terrorífica, y dentro de aquel vacío, ¡quién sabe si se esconde un alma!...Todo podría ser. Los de a caballo, embrazando la adarga, en actitud de torneo más que de guerra, tomaríanse por inmensos juguetes, que fueron solaz de la Historia cuando era niña...En alguno de los guerreros de a pie, cuando ya la luz del día determinaba por entero sus formas, podía observarse que los maniquíes vestidos del pesado traje de acero se aburrían soberanamente, hartos ya de la inmovilidad que desencajaba sus músculos de cartón, y del plumero que les limpiaba la cara un sábado y otro, en miles de semanas. Las manos podridas, con algún dedo de menos, y los demás tiesos, no habrían podido sostener la lanza o el mandoble si no se les ataran con un tosco bramante. En lo alto de aquel lindo museo, las banderas blancas con la cruz de San Andrés colgaban mustias, polvorosas, deshilachadas, recordando los tiempos felices en que ondeaban al aire en las bizarras galeras del Tirreno y del Adriático.

Del riquísimo archivo se posesionó la claridad matutina en un abrir de ojos o de ventanas. En la cavidad espaciosa, de elevado techo, fría como un panteón y solitaria como templo de la sabiduría, rara vez entraba persona viviente, fuera del criado encargado de la limpieza y de algún erudito escudriñador de rarezas bibliográficas. La estantería, de alambradas puertas, cubría toda la pared hasta la escocia, y por los huequecillos de la red metálica confusamente se distinguían lomos de pergamino, cantos de ceñidos legajos amarillentos, y formas diversas de papelería. Al entrar la vigilante luz retirábase cauteloso a su domicilio el ratón más trasnochador de aquellas soledades: contento y ahito iba el muy tuno, seguido de toda la familia, pues entre padres, hijos, sobrinos y nietos, se habían cenado en amor y compaña una de las más interesantes cartas del Gran Capitán al Rey Católico y parte de un curiosísimo *Inventario de alhajas y cuadros*, pertenecientes al virrey de Nápoles, don Pedro Téllez Girón, *el Grande de Osuna*. Estos y otros escandalosos festines ocurrían por haberse muerto de cólico miserere el gato que allí campaba y no haberse cuidado los señores de proveer la plaza, nombrando nuevo gato o gobernador de aquellos oscuror reinos. (v. 1112)

The introduction to *Torquemada y San Pedro* employs some of the same techniques as that of *La de Bringas*, but the text is not as convoluted. Rather Galdós is moving to a more transcendental concept of irony, whose images are broader and more symbolic, in harmony with the more extended prose. The subject of the description seems to demand a more elevated sentiment of irony than does a hair-cenotaph, and so does the story of a man's eternal salvation or perdition. Accordingly, the scene appears to provide a more broadly comprehensive vision than that of *La de Bringas*. Rather than scrutinizing each hair (like Bringas) the narrator is more distanced, and enumerates the objects of the room as they appear illuminated by the morning sun. The narrator seems to disappear, leaving only an occasional reflexive object to indicate the act of observation ('podía observarse'). This rather impressionistic effect – where the narrator's view and his telling coincide with the sun's illumination – reflects the reader's progressive perception of the ironic significance in this scene and of the novel.[2] The description pertains to the protagonist himself: the light of dawn which enters the former palace of Gravelinas symbolizes the light of awareness which seeks to invade the present owner of the edifice, Torquemada. The light symbolizes San Pedro, as Torquemada calls the priest who tries to save his soul. But the symbolic code to which this name belongs also admits an ironic counterpart: San Pedro can be represented by the image in the final sentence of the 'gato o gobernador de aquellos oscuros reinos'. This comparison to a 'gato' points to the ambiguous role which San Pedro, like Torquemada, plays in the novel. In light of the varied connotations of 'cat', San Pedro's 'governing' of Torquemada may be ironic; 'gato' suggests a thief or a money-bag as well as a guard against mice and rats.[3] The 'oscuros reinos' of the palace also allude to those which exist inside Torquemada, and within his personified treasures. They become interchangeable as images of darkness, desertion, neglect, and perhaps soullessness. The dichotomies of this novel begin with the title itself, *Torquemada y San Pedro*, which invokes the antitheses of hell and heaven, dark and light, ruin and treasure, mice and cats, all of which are ironically interdependent, and whose codes eventually merge. The climactic effect of the spreading light is thwarted by its illumination of those who destroy, the mice. This foretells the ironical cumulative structure of Torquemada's phenomenal financial and social success, which ends in his physical and linguistic ruin; his health decays, his speech and his wanderings return to the locus of his usury. The language of this introductory setting displays this structure: first it employs a stylized and somewhat archaic syntax and vocabulary which fit its subject, the treasures of history; finally the description comes to rest in the farthest corner of the room – on the 'ratones'. They are the lowly, filthy creatures who (like Torquemada) are content to defile the treasures of the past: 'El ratón... contento y ahito iba el muy tuno, pues entre padres, hijos, sobrinos y nietos, se habían cenado en amor y compaña una de las más interesantes cartas del Gran Capitán al Rey Católico.' Torquemada's monstrously retarded son will continue the consuming decay of his relatives. The descent of language to the colloquial here evokes the ironic incongruity of wealth and ruin, of earthly treasure and otherworldly reward.

The *claroscuro* effect is achieved in these paragraphs through the light which invades the shadow – both aspects are personified and symmetrically aligned. The first words, 'las primeras claridades', contrast with the last, 'aquellos oscuros reinos'. The first sentence inscribes its own irony in its symmetrical antitheses, and mirrors the structure of the rest of the passage and of the novel. The main verb, 'iba despertando', divides the subject and the terms of light, 'primeras claridades ...amanecer...claraboyas...tragaluces', from the predicate and the terms of darkness, 'sueño de la oscuridad, nada negra'. The process of awakening to a 'vida pictórica' metaphorically defines the process of the narration itself which gradually unfolds its meaning, and the phrase emphasizes the impressionistic quality of the passage. The 'toque de color' and other pictorial terminology reinforce the text's definition of its own picturesque effect and its merger of the arts; the style of description reflects its subject. The objects in the room, valuable arms and armour, representing epochs, warriors and kings past – 'inmensos juguetes que fueron solaz de la Historia cuando era niña' – are all set forth in their own archaic prose. They now rest motionless, wearied and disintegrating in the 'oscuros reinos' of a palace owned by a dying usurer who incarnates the decline of the values and language of the past. The ruin of history is personified in its decaying relics, which in turn personify Torquemada. Like the armour, he too may whimsically be suspected of bearing a soul hidden within his shell. The final sentences of the novel suspend the ironic fluctuation of these paragraphs and of the whole novel in ambiguity when Torquemada dies uttering the word 'conversión'. It may refer either to the salvation of his soul, or to his lasting obsession with the external and material trappings of wealth. That such wealth rots in his possession is a comment on the social status and function of a usurer. The dual significance of the word 'conversión' underscores the dichotomy which informs the novel at many levels. The final irony is that we are not told which meaning is correct and thus we confront the ultimate goal of irony, which never ceases working to undermine belief in absolutes.

Nazarín

A un periodista de los de nuevo cuño, de estos que designamos con el exótico nombre de *reporter*, de estos que corren tras la información, como el galgo a los alcances de la liebre, y persiguen el incendio, la bronca, el suicidio, el crimen cómico o trágico, el hundimiento de un edificio y cuantos sucesos afectan al orden público y a la Justicia en tiempos comunes, o a la higiene en días de epidemia, debo el descubrimiento de la casa de huéspedes de la *tía Chanfaina* (en la fe de bautismo *Estefanía*), situada en una calle cuya mezquindad y pobreza contrastan del modo más irónico con su altísono y coruscante nombre: calle de las Amazonas. Los que no estén hechos a la eterna *guasa* de Madrid, la ciudad (o villa) del sarcasmo y las mentiras maleantes, no pararán mientes en la tremenda fatuidad que supone rótulo tan sonoro en calle tan inmunda, ni se detendrán a investigar qué amazonas fueron esas que la bautizaron, ni de dónde vinieron, ni qué demonios se les había perdido en los Madroñales del Oso. He aquí un *vacío* que mi erudición se apresura a llenar, manifestando con orgullo de sagaz cronista que en aquellos lugares hubo en tiempos de Maricastaña un corral de la villa, y que de él salieron a caballo, aderezadas a estilo de las heroínas mitológicas, unas comparsas de mujeronas que concurrieron a los festejos con que celebró Madrid la entrada de la reina doña Isabel de Valois. Y dice el ingenuo *avisador* coetáneo, a quien debo estas profundas sabidurías: 'Aquellas hembras, buscadas *ad hoc*, hicieron prodigios de valor en las plazas y calles de la villa, por lo arriesgado de sus juegos, equilibrios y volteretas, figurando los guerreros cogerlas del cuello y arrancarlas del arzón para precipitarlas en el suelo.' Memorable debió de ser este divertimiento, porque el corral se llamó desde entonces de las Amazonas, y aquí tenéis el glorioso abolengo de la calle, ilustrada en nuestros días por el establecimiento hospitalario y benéfico de la *tía Chanfaina*.

Tengo yo para mí que las amazonas de que habla el cronista de Felipe II, muy señor mío, eran unas desvergonzadas chulapas del siglo XVI; más no sé con qué vocablo las designaba entonces el vulgo. Lo que sí puedo asegurar es que desciende de ellas, por línea de bastardía, o sea por sucesión directa de hembras marimachos sin padre conocido, la terrible *Estefanía la del Peñón, Chanfaina,* o como demonios se llame. Porque digo con toda verdad que se me despega la pluma, cuando quiero aplicárselo, el apacible nombre de mujer, y que me bastará dar conocimiento a mis lectores de su facha, andares, vozarrón, lenguaje y modos para que reconozcan en ella la más formidable tarasca que vieron los antiguos Madriles y esperan ver los venideros.

No obstante, me pueden creer que doy gracias a Dios, y al reportero, mi amigo, por haberme encarado con aquella fiera, pues debo a su barbarie el germen de la presente historia y el hallazgo del singularísimo personaje que le da nombre. No tome nadie al pie de la letra lo de *casa de huéspedes* que al principio se ha dicho, pues entre las varias industrias de alojamiento que la *tía Chanfaina* ejercía en aquel rincón, y las del centro de Madrid, que todos hemos conocido en la edad estudiantil, y aun después de ella, no hay otra semejanza que la del nombre. El portal del edificio era como de mesón, ancho, con todo el revoco desconchado en mil fantásticos dibujos, dejando ver aquí y allí el hueco de la pared desnudo y con una faja de suciedad a un lado y otro, señal del roce continuo de personas más que de caballerías. Un puesto de bebidas – botellas y garrafas...–reducía la entrada a proporciones regulares. El patio, mal empedrado y peor barrido...era de una irregularidad, más que pintoresca, fantástica. El lienzo del Sur debió de pertenecer a los antiguos edificios del corral famoso; lo demás, de diferentes épocas, pudiera pasar por una broma arquitectónica:...por un lado, pies derechos carcomidos sustentando una galería que se inclina como un barco varado; por otro, puertas de cuarterones con gateras tan grandes que por ellas cabrían tigres si allí los hubiese; rejas de color de canela; trozos de ladrillo amoratado, como coágulos de sangre; y, por fin, los escarceos de la luz y la sombra en todos aquellos ángulos cortantes y oquedades siniestras.

. . .

Subimos, al fin, deseando ver todos los escondrijos de la extraña mansión, guarida de una tan fecunda y lastimosa parte de la Humanidad, y en un cuartucho, cuyo piso de rotos baldosines imitaba en las subidas y bajadas a las olas de un proceloso mar, vimos a Estefanía en chancletas, lavándose las manazas, que después se enjugó en su delantal de harpillera; la panza voluminosa, los brazos hercúleos, el seno emulando en proporciones a la barriga y cargando sobre ella, por no avenirse con apreturas de corsé; el cuello ancho, carnoso y con un morrillo como el de un toro; la cara encendida y con restos bien marcados de una belleza de brocha gorda, abultada, barroca, llamativa, como la de una ninfa de pintura de techos, dibujada para ser vista de lejos, y que se ve de cerca. (v. 1679–81)

The first chapter of *Nazarín*, the chronicle of an unorthodox priest who goes into the countryside to imitate Christ's suffering, like many other introductory passages in Galdós' work, incorporates the codes of irony which will traverse the entire novel. The irony of a quixotic Christ, a saintly madman, is considered from many angles in *Nazarín*, just as the many facets of this edifice are viewed in these first pages. The story and its language invoke the mythic and the ridiculous, the exotic and the banal. As a chronicle, it parodies itself and *Don Quijote*, from which it draws many other ironies as well.[4] Like Don Quijote, Nazarín views life from a different perspective, and, depending on our own, his seems either sublime or ridiculous, clear-sighted or blind. The architecture of the building and the portrait of its owner, Estefanía, describe and inscribe the ironic structure of the whole novel, which becomes a game in prose, as the building is 'una broma arquitectónica'. This edifice, like Nazarín's mind and the story of his adventures, is a contrast of light and shadow: 'los escarceos de la luz y la sombra en todos aquellos ángulos cortantes y oquedades siniestras'. It is only through the contrast that one can perceive that all is not the same, that all is not surface, and that the figurative is in ironic opposition to the literal. The last words of the chapter conclude the description of Estefanía and delineate this process of perception: 'la cara encendida y con restos bien marcados de una belleza de brocha gorda, abultada, barroca, llamativa, como la de una ninfa de pintura de techos, dibujada para ser vista de lejos, y que se ve de cerca'. Her beauty evades the closer regard, as when an impressionist painting is viewed too closely. Likewise, the metaphor must not be interpreted literally or it will lose its reality, which is ultimately figurative and indescribable – like beauty. This perspective on Estefanía, Nazarín's perspective, and the reader's are all parallel. Through them Galdós presents the novel, which again deals with the irony of reality and appearance. The irony extends particularly to the act of reading *Nazarín*; if the reader fixes on either the accuracy or the distortion of the history which Nazarín's visions are said to constitute he may confuse its meaning. Although the ugly Estefanía is the owner of a brothel, she appears beautiful if one looks beyond her environment and 'face value' to her genuine charity toward Nazarín.

From the beginning we are offered a text which calls explicit attention to its irony. Again the first sentence anticipates the rest of the passage, the novel, and the process of perceiving its irony. The sentence is divided in half by the main verb, 'debo', and employs a symmetrical alternation of allusive codes. The pedantically literary is juxtaposed to the colloquial, the exotic and mythic to the ridiculous and vulgar. The sentence moves from the elaborate description of the 'periodista...con el exótico nombre de *reporter*', to a comic simile of him 'como un galgo a los alcances de la liebre'. There is an explicit invocation of an alternation between the 'cómico o trágico' found in the journalist's work, which thus insinuates a commentary on the narrative of *Nazarín*. The rhyme of 'hundimiento' and 'descubrimiento' brackets the main verb 'debo'. Then, in the naming of 'la *tía Chanfaina*', the tone changes again, reflecting the *trágico–cómico* irony which the novel shares with *Don Quijote* and the New Testament. The irony of the 'calle mezquina' and 'su altísono y coruscante nombre' is overt. The sentence ends in a mythic, literary reference, 'amazonas'. The first noun of this sentence, 'periodista', also initiates the implied parody of the chronicle. The ensuing alternation between the codes of discourse is repeated throughout the chapter and is often expressly noted, as in 'la tremenda fatuidad que supone rótulo tan sonoro en calle tan inmunda' in the second sentence, where the fluctuation of the literary and the colloquial continues: 'investigar qué amazonas fueron esas' contrasts with 'ni qué demonios se les había perdido'. The cumulative ironic effect achieved from both inversion and vocabulary is evident throughout. The third sentence moves from the terms 'erudición', 'manifestar', 'sagaz cronista', and 'heroínas mitológicas' to 'unas comparsas de mujeronas'. The fourth employs an oscillating movement: an 'ingenuo *avisador*' offers 'profundas sabidurías' beginning with 'aquellas hembras', which is in turn qualified by the pedantic '*ad hoc*'. The last sentence of the first paragraph employs another ironic anticlimax as it speaks of the 'memorable divertimiento', 'glorioso abolengo', 'establecimiento hospitalario y benéfico' – of 'la *tía Chanfaina*'. The mixture of erudite chronicle and colloquial account pervades these paragraphs and the entire text; *Nazarín* is a parody of *Don Quijote*, of itself as a pretended chronicle, and of historical, mythological, naturalistic (through an implicit reference to Zola's concept of the novelist as an investigative reporter), and even biblical literature.

Through irony, the reader recognizes that things are not what they seem, and that this language, with its contrast between signifiers and banal signifieds, does not describe anything precisely. In the same manner he realizes that there is more to the novel than 'meets the eye'. In other words, the novel is not just the story of a quixotic Christ – it is a quest for ideals and perhaps a picture of vanity and egoism.[5] Like *Don Quijote*, it is a lesson in reading fiction and reality. We learn that even the deeper meaning, the ironic *vraisemblance*, may not be the final truth. In the third paragraph the narrator tells us that the 'establecimiento hospitalario' which is really a 'casa de huéspedes' is not even that, but rather a brothel. The narrator's advice, 'no tome nadie al pie de la letra lo de *casa de huéspedes* que al principio se ha dicho...no hay otra semejanza que la del nombre' is not a figurative expression alone here, but a literal warning of how to read the language of this novel. One must see beyond the language of appearance, beyond the 'nombres' and 'rótulos', to another meaning which stands at an ironic angle – like the angles of the edifice – to their expression. This applies not only to this text, but also to Madrid and its readers. The city itself is ironic: 'la eterna *guasa* de Madrid, la ciudad (o villa) del sarcasmo y las mentiras maleantes'. The parenthetical 'o villa' marks the irony of Madrid's pretension to be a city; raised from humble origins by royal aggrandizement, it does not yet have a cathedral. Names, as language, are ironic façades; their appearances are masks of reality. Likewise, the novel does not pretend to make truth or reality present, but may, through irony, point in its direction by gesturing away from the certainty of subjectivity, whether it is Nazarín's, Quijote's, or the reader's.

Misericordia

Dos caras, como algunas personas, tiene la parroquia de San Sebastián... mejor será decir la iglesia...dos caras que seguramente son más graciosas que bonitas: con la una mira a los barrios bajos, enfilándolos por la calle de Cañizares; con la otra, el señorío mercantil de la plaza del Ángel. Habréis notado en ambos rostros una fealdad risueña, del más puro Madrid, en quien el carácter arquitectónico y el moral se aúnan maravillosamente. En la cara del Sur campea, sobre una puerta chabacana, la imagen barroca del santo mártir, retorcida, en actitud más bien danzante que religiosa; en la del Norte, desnuda de ornatos, pobre y vulgar, se alza la torre, de la cual podría creerse que se pone en jarras, soltándole cuatro frescas en la plaza del Ángel. Por una y otra banda, las caras o fachadas tienen anchuras, quiere decirse, patios cercados de verjas mohosas, y en ellos tiestos con lindos arbustos, y un mercadillo de flores que recrea la vista. En ninguna parte como aquí advertiréis el encanto, la simpatía, el *ángel*, dicho sea en andaluz, que despiden de sí, como tenue fragancia, las cosas vulgares, o algunas de las infinitas cosas vulgares que hay en el mundo. Feo y pedestre como un pliego de aleluyas o como los romances de ciego, el edificio bifronte, con su torre *barbiana*, el capulín de la capilla de la Novena, los irregulares techos y cortados muros, con su afeite barato de ocre, sus patios floridos, sus hierros mohosos en la calle y en el alto campanario, ofrece un conjunto gracioso, picante, *majo*, por decirlo de una vez. Es un rinconcito de Madrid que debemos conservar cariñosamente, como anticuarios coleccionistas, porque la caricatura monumental también es un arte. Admiremos en este San Sebastián, heredado de los tiempos viejos, la estampa ridícula y tosca, y guardémoslo como un lindo mamarracho.

Con tener honores de puerta principal, la del Sur es la menos favorecida de fieles en días ordinarios, mañana y tarde. Casi todo el señorío entra por la del Norte, que más parece puerta excusada o familiar. Y no necesitaremos hacer estadística de los feligreses que acuden al sagrado culto por una parte y otra, porque tenemos un *contador* infalible: los pobres. Mucho más numerosa y formidable que por el Sur es por el Norte la cuadrilla de miseria que acecha el paso de la caridad, al modo de guardia de alcabaleros que cobra humanamente el portazgo en la frontera de lo divino, o la contribución impuesta a las conciencias impuras, que van a donde lavan. (v. 1877)

Misericordia, to many readers, represents Galdós' highest single artistic achievement; surely it is one of his best novels. His ironic style has reached its most subtle refinement in various ways. Robert Russell has illustrated how the novel is a structure of ironies in which hunger becomes a blessing, blindness vision, servant master, madness wisdom, and illusion reality.[6] The union of these opposites is displayed at many levels of this novel, and most succinctly in the introductory description of the church of San Sebastián. The first two paragraphs of the novel reveal such perfection of ironic intertextuality that the architecture portrayed becomes the architecture of the language of description, of the portrait of the heroine, of the Madrid of the novel, and of the novelesque structure as a totality. The faces of San Sebastián describe Benina and Madrid, whose beauty and ugliness ironically coexist. The first sentence is divided into three sections by a colon and semicolon, and the first four clauses of the first section enumerate four levels of meaning, each an ironic comment on the one preceding. The aside, 'mejor será decir iglesia', calls attention not to the 'iglesia' it mentions, but rather to the various applications of 'parroquia' to the people as well as the building and neighborhood. The simile, 'como algunas personas', sharpens the personification suggested by the metaphorical aside 'dos caras'. This aside makes explicit the irony of the other face, or of the 'señorío' of the parish. It functions in the same ways as does the reference to 'la caridad', in the last sentence of the passage, which is redefined as 'la contribución impuesta a las conciencias impuras, que van a donde lavan'. These two clarifying asides form the beginning and end of the description of the church, and complete the circular structure of meanings. These passages expose an hypocrisy which itself is an intrinsically ironic phenomenon: two opposites (two faces, two meanings) existing in the same body. The ironic duality which pervades these paragraphs is underscored by a prose filled with repetition, parallel sentence structure, and pairs of images. The parallel syntax is reinforced in the first sentence by the anaphoric 'dos caras', and by the isocolon 'con la una...con la otra'. The south façade is never mentioned without the north one being described, and their appearances, like their topographical positions, are contradictory. The personification of the church is established not only through the continued use of 'rostros' and 'caras', but also through adjectives, verbs, clauses, and figures of speech describing their architectural attitudes. The description also ironically foreshadows the story, as in the remark 'en la del Norte, desnuda de ornatos, pobre y vulgar...podría creerse que se pone en jarras'. This back door serves the wealthy merchant classes, and the colloquially expressed indignation reflects that of the 'señorío mercantil' toward Benina. The lack of ornament symbolizes Juliana, don Carlos Trujillo, and other hypocrites who lack true virtue. The terms 'pobre' and 'vulgar' indicate that the external characteristics of Benina and other poor beggars are the internal attributes of the 'señorío mercantil'.

San Sebastián is like Madrid, we are told, 'en quien el carácter arquitectónico y el moral se aúnan maravillosamente'. The choice of 'quien' confirms the extension of the church to personify the people of Madrid. And this statement explicitly describes the identity of the structure of the prose with its message. The description of San Sebastián embraces and foreshadows the themes of the novel: the hypocrisy and charity, ugliness and beauty, which become ironic in their juxtaposition. Just as the two façades would not be ironic if they did not belong to the same church, such themes would not be so incongruent if they were not embodied in the same character. The term 'maravillosamente' is more than figurative, too, because the story becomes fantastic as Benina's mental creation of Don Romualdo becomes a novelesque reality. Besides this thematic connotation, the word 'maravillosamente' indicates that the novelesque reality is still an illusion. Just as the 'carácter arquitectónico y el moral' are marvelously joined in San Sebastián and Madrid, so they are in the novel. A marvelous fusion becomes an ironic one, because things are not what they seem.

Language does not encompass or unite with meaning, it only points towards it. Because of the multiple meanings possible in any expression, language is the archetypal ironist that 'says one thing and means another', and whose reality is always illusion.

The appearance of the church is also that of Benina; both possess 'una fealdad risueña'. This oxymoron, as well as the phrase 'lindo mamarracho' at the end of the paragraph, emblemize the irony. An 'edificio' or 'persona' may be 'feo y pedestre' while still retaining a 'conjunto gracioso, picante, *majo*'. 'Las cosas vulgares, o algunas de las infinitas cosas vulgares que hay en el mundo' possess 'el encanto, la simpatía, el *ángel*'. The two series of adjectives ending with the personifications '*majo*' and '*ángel*' represent lower-class jargon and are appropriate to Benina's status as *pueblo*. Moreover she is later called an angel by a mad old fool, Ponte, and considered beautiful by the blind Moor, Almudena. The qualification introduced by 'o algunas' extends the image to include Benina and 'el más puro Madrid'.

The story ostensibly concerns Benina's travels between two physically and morally opposed neighbourhoods. But because she embodies ironic codes of meaning, Benina becomes the instrument through which these codes traverse and shape the characters, plot, and themes of the entire novel. Her movement in the lower topographical levels of the novel allows her mistress, Doña Paca, to rise; as Benina descends even lower, she progressively displays an ever more perfect moral composition. The church door facing the poor districts of Madrid is adorned with an image of 'el santo mártir' portrayed 'en actitud más bien danzante que religiosa'. The use of qualifications such as 'más bien que' or 'más graciosa que bonita' (a kind of *correctio* or metanoia) is continual in the novel, and calls attention to the persistent multiplicity of meaning. The attitude of 'el santo mártir' is also Benina's, and perhaps points to a message of the novel; her frenzied charitable activities are not consciously pious, nor is the 'moral' of this novel as conventionally religious as it may seem. Benina lies, bribes, hoards, and perhaps even steals (although ultimately only from herself) in order to further her charity. And she is not without momentary resentment for those who are ungrateful to her. Neither her charity nor her suffering is Christ-like in a literal sense, but rather in an ironic, figurative sense. A figure, like a metaphor, both is and is not itself; Benina is and is not Christ-like and while she is ultimately only a linguistic structure, she seems to embrace a meaning that transcends her.

Misericordia shows that the *misericordia* of Benina is ironic, for she

displays both virtue and vice in nearly all her acts: 'difícil expresar
dónde se empalmaban y confundían la virtud y el vicio' (v. 1895).
Robert Kirsner believes that 'cuando se corre la cortina moral [del
libro], se discierne el proceso creativo del artista. Se puede ver entonces
al titiritero sonriéndose mientras que juega con sus muñecas para
ilusionar al público.'[7] Just as in the church of San Sebastián, the moral
and architectural aspects of the novel – its meaning and its language –
are 'marvelously', but not truly, fused; for they are always ironically
opposed. In the illusory nature of language itself lies, perhaps, the final
irony: that there is no escape from it. Yet Benina, like San Sebastián,
transcends the differences within her life. Just as two very different
faces exist in the same building, because the church is open to all, so
Benina endures the most diverse fortunes, because she makes no judgment between them. Her love, like the Christian ideal, is not discriminating. To her everything, even money or hunger, is from God.
If she does see hypocrisy, uselessness, or ingratitude in the individuals
around her, she still continues to love those people, simply because even
they too are God's creatures. Irony can only exist in difference, but to
Benina, just as to her God, all is the same.

These four opening scenes inscribe the structures of the complete
novels in many ways – through their linguistic composition, suggestive
imagery, and the reader's perception of meaning. This is true of
Galdós' novels from the polemical *Doña Perfecta* to the fantastic *El
caballero encantado*. Other settings also contain these levels of ironic
specularity, though often not so obviously or concisely. Almost each
narrative passage can, however, be viewed in some way as a reflection
of itself, of other passages, of the entire novel, and of the act of its
reading. The irony which organizes such scenes at each of these levels
is the irony of the approximation to reality of perception and language.[8]

3

The narrator of irony

Scholars of many critical stances have discussed how the position of the narrator affects the reading, and therefore the meaning, of a novel. One role of the narrator has already been examined in his creation of ironic portraits. We have seen how his voice fades in and out of the text by means of such devices as the free indirect style, omniscient narration, first-person asides, apostrophe, and indirect parentheses to the reader. This voice, interjected at crucial points in the text, serves to illuminate and sometimes to obscure irony. If we view the narrator conventionally as the means through which we must pass to 'reach' the characters, then it is also through this construct of the text that irony must pass. For it is the voice of the narrator that seems to direct our reading by indicating where we should focus our attention. Summarizing various critical analyses of this process, Culler writes: 'As the image of the narrator begins to emerge, that of an imaginary reader is also sketched. The narrative indicates what he needs to be told, how he might have reacted, what deductions or connections he is presumed to accept' (*Structuralist Poetics*, p. 195). This conventional formation of a contract between a differentiated narrator and the reader constitutes the 'voice of reading' defined by Barthes. When this voice is inaudible or misleading, then the contract dissolves and the text becomes problematic.

The free indirect style is one means by which the voice of reading becomes nearly inaudible because of the difficulty of deciding 'who is speaking'. This obstacle to determining the guiding voice can lead to the reader's being ironized if he identifies the voice incorrectly. Obscurity is not the only factor which contributes to an ironic voice of reading, however. For if the narrator, whose words are often conventionally accepted as those of novelistic truth, is instead deceived or purposely deceitful, the deductions or connections which he offers to the reader are ironic. Again, if the reader accepts them as true, he becomes a victim of that irony.

We naturalize a novel, or make it intelligible, through both the narrator and the 'shape' or generic identity of the text as a narrative form. Our reading is determined not only by 'point of view' (or the apparent lack of it), but also by the way a text presents itself: as a document of social reality, a fantasy, an autobiography, history, or as an epistolary or dialogue novel, to name but a few types. Whether the narration is more historical or discursive will also influence our reading by lengthening or shortening the distance between us and the events or characters. The same effects are achieved by the narrator's degree of assumed familiarity with us, or with the characters. The illusion of a totally absent narrator, no less than that of an omnipresent one, cannot but contribute to our understanding of the novel. In general, then, our expectations of, and conclusions about, the novel are always modified by the position of the narrator, the temporal structure of the text, and the conventions of genre – of 'form and content' – which it invokes. The reader draws on the conventions with which he is already familiar and applies them to the novel he is reading. When familiar novelistic conventions are twisted or extended in some way, irony arises and forces the reader to re-evaluate the conventional literary – and ultimately cultural – connotations of the novel.

Galdós' use of novelistic conventions throughout the *Novelas contemporáneas* displays extensive experimentation and innovation. We have already observed, for example, how *La desheredada* incorporates an extended parody of the *folletín* and of *Don Quijote*. Besides the various modes of narration noted so far, different types of narrators (including the character–narrator) also appear, each possessing a different degree of 'knowledge about' and 'activity within' the text. The epistolary form, the historical chronicle, and the dialogue novel are employed singly and together throughout the series. These variations all offer new types and degrees of irony, and especially lead to new insights into where irony lies and how it comes to be perceived. As these novels present themselves to the reader, they also direct his awareness of irony at all levels of perception and interpretation.

Galdós continually and progressively subverts the appeal to an objective point of view. The analyses of character and setting have illustrated this subversion at work. The perspectives of Isidora and Rosalía are undermined, and the hyperbolic language used to describe 'el tal cenotafio de pelo' is just as much of a distortion as the picture which it supposedly describes. This ironic approach to objectivity also functions

at the level of the narrator. The convention of the chronicle in particular, by recalling *Don Quijote*, recalls its play with the role of the
narrator, and with the objectivity of truth and history. In *La desheredada*, the first novel of the series, the chronicle device is alluded to in
such references as 'los documentos de que se ha formado esta historia'.
This allusion is significant not only because of the parodic effect which
it displays (in a multiple sense).[1] It is also a signal to the reader to keep
his distance from the fictional Isidora, because it ironically affirms her
non-historical status. This is one end which the chronicle always serves:
it reveals fictionality by claiming history. The use of this device cul-
minates in a work like *Nazarín*, which has been ironically 'filtered'
through the successive redactions of the investigative reporter, his
friend, the marvelous transcriber, and, of course, the hidden narrator
and implied author. *Nazarín* displays the same 'filtering process' that
occurs in the 'historical' transcription of *Don Quijote* by the *segundo
autor*, the translator, Cide Hamete, and the ultimate controlling hand
of the implied author.[2] The prologue-like Part 1 of *Nazarín* ends by
invoking this illusive narrative hierarchy:

Lo que a renglón seguido se cuenta, ¿es verídica historia, o una invención
de esas que por la doble virtud del arte expeditivo de quien las escribe, y la
credulidad de quien las lee, resultan como una ilusión de la realidad?
Y oigo, además, otras preguntas: '¿Quién demonios ha escrito lo que
sigue? ¿Ha sido usted, el reportero, o la *tía Chanfaina*, o el gitano
viejo?...' Nada puedo contestar, porque yo mismo me vería muy confuso
si tratara de determinar quién ha escrito lo que escribo. No respondo del
procedimiento; sí respondo de la exactitud de los hechos. El narrador se
oculta. La narración, nutrida de sentimiento de las cosas y de histórica
verdad, se manifiesta en sí misma, clara, precisa, sincera. (v. 1691)

This pretense of absolute fictional autonomy within the realm of
history is thoroughly self-contradictory, and it forces the reader to
participate either knowingly or unknowingly in its irony. For while the
experienced reader – especially of *Don Quijote* – may realize that
Nazarín is fictional, the very act of affirming that fictionality may lead
him to forget that the 'yo' of the narrator (who doubles himself in
'usted') and of the reporter are just as fictional as Cide Hamete and
the *segundo autor* of the *Quijote*. This is the basis for the irony of the
'novel within the novel'; while thinking that the 'inner' presentation
is more fictional, we usually forget that the 'outer' structure – conventionally considered as mediating and therefore more 'real' – is just
as fictional. As Barthes has suggested, there is no such thing as a fiction

within a fiction; all is language.[3] Only our conventions of reading create this separation, just as we postulate the existence of characters. This same ironic 'Chinese-box' illusion occurs within *Misericordia*, a 'verídica historia', where Benina seems to create another character, Don Romualdo, from her imagination. This becomes a reflection of, and a putative equation with, Galdós' own creative process; Don Romualdo and Benina are both like Dulcinea, but without Aldonza Lorenzo. The novels *Nazarín* and *Halma* also contain this ironic nesting structure and constitute rewritings at many levels of *Don Quijote* Parts I and II, respectively. Nazarín in the novel of that name is an 'author' while he becomes an 'actor' in *Halma*, for example. In *Nazarín*, he wanders about the plains, seeing divine opportunity in mendicancy and plague and converting squire-like followers. In *Halma*, Nazarín comes to Halma's *torre* where she and others attempt to direct his behavior, just as that of Don Quijote was directed at the ducal palace. Nazarín is another actor–author, *loco–cuerdo* like Don Quijote; but unlike him, Nazarín never renounces his illusions. He is perhaps more quixotic than Quijote. The narrative supports this ultimate *quijotismo* of Nazarín because the narrator pretends to believe in his illusions (whereas the narrator of *Don Quijote* clearly states that the windmills are windmills), and no 'realistic' dénouement takes place. Each possibly 'rational' explanation for Nazarín's actions is ironically subverted, even at the end. The last 'historical' note concerning Nazarín (in the last lines of *Halma*) is based on 'un curiosísimo documento nazarista'. While still pretending to be historical and objective – though of course in an ironic way – this later *novela contemporánea* (in two parts) has left the realm of putative reality and morality to which the earlier *La desheredada* seems to have reference; Nazarín's life does not appear to reflect any conventional reality.

It is obvious that Galdós' debt to and development of Cervantes' work extends in some way to almost every level of his novelistic creation. He not only employs multiple narrators and ironic historical references in order to reveal fictions's fictionality, but also applies more subtle devices as well, such as the 'phantom chapters' phenomenon which Raymond Willis has discussed with regard to *Don Quijote*. Willis has shown how characteristic syntactic and stylistic oddities at the beginning and end of most chapters work to dissolve the conventional notion of a uniform, logical organization of the novel's content. Form and content are instead one flowing substance, like life itself, which cannot be divided by any 'logical' system.[4] Extending Willis' analysis, one might observe that this dissolution of the chapter divisions is a reflection of the ultimately continuous – but arbitrarily divided – process of perceiving the difference between reality and fiction. Willis' observations apply well to Galdós' *Novelas contemporáneas*, particularly the later works in the series. Throughout these novels, the chapter divisions often seem arbitrary, coming in the middle of a description or of a conversation. But even more, this subversion of the conventions of chapter (or subchapter) sometimes involves determined syntactic or stylistic constructions which force the reader beyond the end of a chapter, instead of providing him with the usual pause. At the beginning of a chapter they at once push his attention back to the previous ending. Such constructions are frequent in *Ángel Guerra* (1890–1), for example. The beginning of Part I, chapter I, section ii, reads: 'De la cual salió súbitamente.' This refers to the close of the previous section in which Guerra 'no tardó en caer en un sopor, que más bien parecía borrachera' (v. 1203). The first division at the level of sub-chapter in *Ángel Guerra* sets the mood for the story of his dreams and illusions which are apparently continuous with the 'historical' portions of the fiction. The reader is almost unable, until the end, to distinguish Guerra's desires from his rational thoughts, and from the 'voice of truth'. The transition between the first two chapters alludes further to the problem of distinguishing reality from fiction:

La familia de Dulce...es digna de pasar a la Historia; pero el narrador necesita curarse en salud, diciendo que los *Babeles*...son de todo punto inverosímiles, lo cual no quita que sean verdaderos. Queda, pues, el lector en libertad de creer o no lo que se cuenta, y aunque esto se tache de imposturas, allá va el retrato con toda la mentira de su verdad, sin quitar ni poner nada a lo increíble ni a lo inconcuso.

CAPITULO II

Los Babeles

Residencia: *Molino de Viento, 32, duplicado*, cuarto que llamaban segundo con efectividad de quinto...El interior resultaba digno molde de la inverosímil familia...(v. 1216)

Don Quijote, and the entire problematics of illusion and reality, are invoked in these paragraphs at every level from the linguistic to the symbolic. 'La mentira de su verdad' describes not only the narration, but perhaps any claim to absolute truth.

Willis concludes his study of *Don Quijote* with a statement (p. 117) applicable to Galdós:

In the *Quijote*, unlike the chivalric, the Pastoral, or the Picaresque Romances [where the structure of the life of the character and that of the narrative are basically congruent and both have an orderly form], the ambient world has many structures; everything in it is as it is seen or felt by every different person in the book (and the author and reader too); and there is no single, real, or thematic, reality that runs throughout. Each reality is at the same time relative and valid. And even the personages are constantly remaking themselves, for the only constant is the will to be.

This, I would propose, is the 'imagen de la vida' that Galdós also seeks to reveal. The Cervantine reflections in these novels are so numerous that they almost defy thorough analysis, yet their import is clear. Like Cervantes, Galdós shows us that the narrative is a continual flow of language within which we construct the conventions of character, plot, theme, fiction, and history. When we label some parts as fiction, we may forget the fictionality of the rest, just as we may label the characters as fictional and forget that the narrator is too. These decisions of ours, which we consider valid, are as arbitrary as any chapter divisions. We should not be too certain of our own objectivity, because the text of the novel (and perhaps of the world) may be ultimately ironic; each meaning conceals another, and the one which appears most absolute may be as relative as the next.

Galdós' use of the first-person narrator has its ironical effects. The first-person plural in *Tormento* and *La de Bringas*, as we saw, forces the reader to participate in the novel and thus to run the risk of becoming a victim of its irony. Even with the first-person singular, we are drawn closer to the characters: when the narrator admits his own proximity to them, ours is implied. This can become highly ironic if the narrator's position of apparent superiority to the characters is undermined. In *La de Bringas* we learn that the narrator is not only a friend of Pez and Bringas, to whom he owes favors, but that he is one of Rosalía's lovers during the periods of the Revolution and the Republic. The narrator performs transitional duties in the government and for Rosalía. The reader's proximity to the narrator brings him to a more 'intimate' relationship with Rosalía and with her appearance-oriented novelistic society.[5] The narrator's position is ultimately undermined by the possibility that he may even be Ido de Sagrario, the writer of *folletines* first encountered in *El doctor Centeno*. In the closing paragraphs the narrator says, 'Francamente, naturalmente, los ví salir con pena.' Shoemaker first pointed out the identity of these words with Ido's.[6] This offers a further ironization of the story's historical and veridical content, and hence of the reader's participation in and evaluation of it.

The narrator's role as character – particularly when this role is limited – can contribute to the reader's belief in the novel's representationalism. If the 'voice of truth' is also a character, he seems to lend a more 'real' aspect to the other characters. As we become more involved in their fiction, the tendency to lend them more of our reality is facilitated by our conventional consideration of the narrator as less fictional than the other characters. The difference appears to dissolve between us and them, reality and fiction; such a process of identification might indicate that our conception of reality is as fictional as we consider the novel to be. When the character-role of the narrator is expanded to that of the protagonist, the distance between the reader and the story closes further, making the reader even more susceptible to ironization. Because we conventionally – or even unknowingly – forget that the narrator is another fictional construction it is easier for us to be deceived by his language than by that of another character's. Yet the narrator is also a reader, and sometimes a misreader, of his own text; his conclusions about himself or others may be intentionally or mistakenly ironic. Galdós makes use of this first-person protagonist–narrator in two of his *Novelas contemporáneas*, *El amigo Manso* (1882) and *Lo prohibido* (1884–5).[7] Both offer further insights into the ironic nature of the concept of objectivity.

A considerable body of often contradictory commentary has been produced in response to the 'mythical' creation of Máximo Manso, which seems to represent the incursion of the fictional into the real.[8] The key to understanding this creation, it appears, lies in the introduction and conclusion to Galdós' prototype of Unamuno's *Niebla*. The strive for autonomy in *El amigo Manso* again explicitly recalls the language of *Don Quijote*. The multiplication of authors in the Prologue to *Don Quijote* Part I occurs in Máximo–autor: 'Tengo yo un amigo que ha incurrido por sus pecados, que deben de ser tantos en número como las arenas de la mar, en la pena infamante de escribir novelas, así como otros cumplen, leyéndolas, la condena o maldición divina. Este tal vino a mí hace pocos días, hablóme de sus trabajos...' (IV. 1165). The denomination 'este tal' especially reinforces the author's ironic self-deprecation in this passage, just as Cervantes did in his Prologue, which he claimed 'to a friend' that he was unable to write. The famed words, 'de cuyo nombre no quiero acordarme', from chapter I of *Don Quijote* are reflected in chapter II of *El amigo Manso*, when Manso tells us that he is a *catedrático* in an *asignatura* 'que no quiero nombrar' (IV. 1166). After swearing that he does not exist in the first paragraph of his novel, Manso describes what he is in the second:

—Soy —diciéndolo en lenguaje oscuro para que lo entiendan mejor— una condensación artística, diabólica hechura del pensamiento humano (*ximia Dei*), el cual, si coge entre sus dedos algo de estilo, se pone a imitar con él las obras que con la materia ha hecho Dios en el mundo físico; soy un ejemplar nuevo de estas falsificaciones del hombre que desde que el mundo es mundo andan por ahí vendidas en tabla por aquellos que yo llamo holgazanes, faltando a todo deber filial, y que el bondadoso vulgo denomina artistas, poetas o cosa así. Quimera soy, sueño de sueño y sombra de sombra... (IV. 1165)

His clarificatory 'lenguaje oscuro' is an emblem of the superation of metaphor by irony; it is both a literal and a figurative reference, yet language is only a figurative and not a literal measure of reality. 'Lenguaje oscuro' allows greater understanding because it seems to distance us from the text; the difference between the thing described and its description becomes more apparent as in the extended example of the hair-cenotaph in *La de Bringas*.[9] From this distance we realize that there are many ways of description, countless approximations of reality. The images of this passage and of the whole first chapter of *El amigo Manso* describe the distance of language from the world. Máximo is an artistic creation of language. Nonetheless he, his novel, artistic style, or even human thought are incapable of being the *materia* 'que ha hecho Dios en el mundo'; they are only 'falsificaciones'. This self-criticism of his own text is specular; it reflects both the self-sufficiency of language when compared to itself, and the deficiency of language when compared to reality. Metaphor cannot be interpreted literally. Some critics claim that this novel is meant to be viewed as an autonomous, self-sufficient thing without necessary reference to reality; the artifice of its own linguistic mechanisms creates it. Yet this limitation embraces the very essence of language; it is an inescapable system, it is 'pensamiento humano', a world unto itself, which can never capture reality, but only supply its surrogates.

The message of the first chapter is the lesson of *El amigo Manso*. Máximo says that his friend was planning to 'perpetrar un detenido crimen novelesco, sobre el gran asunto de la educación', but in the meantime has bought the rights to Manso's story. It appears, however, that the 'novelistic crime' is already underway. *El amigo Manso* is

ostensibly the story of an educator's education. At the same time it
educates the reader in reading the novel, literature and life. Just as
Manso learns that there is no single perspective on life, so we learn that
there is no single novelistic meaning. As the phrase 'un crimen novelesco' suggests, *El amigo Manso* is a parody of the detective story at
many levels. Manso thinks himself an alert observer of society, only to
find that he has been deceived by the surface of things. The reader
eventually discovers that he must read Manso as a deceived narrator,
not as the voice of truth, and finally that there is no single truth; in a
fictional world each perspective will be as credible as the next. *El amigo
Manso* becomes, then, a subversion of realism, of point of view, and of
objectivity. Manso, a 'mythic' figure who becomes 'realistic', maintains
a realistic perspective upon the world of the novel which is revealed as
an illusion. The novel *El amigo Manso* seems to divide myth from
realism in its beginning and end, but instead reaffirms their continuity
as a fiction within language.

Manso repeatedly tells us that his judgments possess a firm base in
reality and that he knows how to perceive the truth of things; he has
this ability because 'desde niño mostré especial querencia a los trabajos especulativos, a la investigación de la verdad y al ejercicio de la
razón' (IV. 1166). He puts this knowledge to use as 'una firme estructura de la realidad de mi vida con poderoso cimiento en mi conciencia'
(IV. 1166). He emphatically affirms his capacity for objective judgment: 'Constantemente me congratulo de este mi carácter templado,
de la condición subalterna de mi imaginación, de mi espíritu observador
y práctico, que me permite tomar las cosas como son realmente, no
equivocarme jamás respecto a su verdadero tamaño, medida y peso y
tener siempre bien tirantes las riendas de mí mismo' (IV. 1169). The
egotism of these words pervades the novel until that *desengaño* in
which Manso discovers that the governess, Irene, is not in love with
him (as he believed), but rather with his young disciple, Peña. This
subjectivity which considers itself objective is linguistically manifested
within the narration. Manso repeatedly emphasizes his *yo* through
redundant use of pronouns in such constructions as 'noté yo' and
'afirmé yo'; in most cases this occurs with verbs of perception. This
reaches great intensity in chapter XVI, whose title, '¿Qué leía usted
anoche?', completes the final sentence of the preceding chapter: 'Sin
oír su respuesta a mi primer saludo, le pregunté:'. Manso had seen
Irene's light burning late at night and believed that she was reading
his philosophical treatises. He relates her response thus:

Y como quien ve descubierto un secreto querido...dijo dos o tres frases evasivas, y a su vez me preguntó no sé qué cosa. Interpreté su turbación de un modo favorable a mi persona, y me dije: 'Quizá leería algo mío.' Pero al punto pensé que no habiendo yo escrito ninguna obra de entretenimiento si algo mío leía...'sin duda —calculé yo— no ha querido decirme que leía estas cosas por no aparecer ante mí como pedantesca o marisabidilla'. (IV. 1204)

His egocentric interpretations extend beyond Irene to everyone, including even his young *sobrinos*: 'Las dos niñas corrieron hacia mí. Eran monísimas, se llamaban mis novias y se disputaban mis besos. Pepito también corrió saltando a mi encuentro' (IV. 1204).

Manso's firm belief in his rational powers and ability to ascertain the truth leads him – and possibly the reader who is deceived by him – into a state of total ignorance about the nature of Irene, Peña, his brother, and even Cándida. But he is most ignorant of himself, whom he thought he knew so thoroughly. Even after Manso realizes that Irene is in love with Peña, he still supposes that he can arrive at the truth because he has subdued his emotional – irrational – side. Instead of studying his ideal woman, whom he calls 'la mujer–razón', he now decides to observe 'la mujer–mujer':

'Quién sabe —me dije— si una crítica completamente sana y fría podría llevarte a declarar que aquellas supuestas, soñadas y rebuscadas perfecciones constituirían, caso de ser reales, el estado más imperfecto del mundo...Eso de la mujer–razón que tanto te entusiasmaba, ¿no será un necio juego del pensamiento? Hay retruécanos de ideas como los hay de palabras...Ponte en el terreno firme de la realidad, y haz un estudio serio de la mujer–mujer...Estos que ahora te parecen defectos, ¿no serán las manifestaciones naturales del temperamento, de la edad, del medio ambiente?...He aquí una huérfana desamparada que se abre camino, y su pasión esconde un genio práctico de primer orden. (IV. 1275–6)

Although he realizes that his previous conclusions about Irene were wrong, he does not consider that this new evaluation of her might also be in error. Despite his romantic disappointment, his self-concept as a 'genio práctico' remains unshaken. But he does find that he cannot ultimately rid himself of emotion: 'cada vez que veía delante de mí a la joven señora de Peña, mujer de mi discípulo, aunque no discípula, sino más bien maestra mía, me entraba tal conjoga y abatimiento que no podía vivir' (IV. 1289). He cannot endure the world, he says, because everything that he believed to be real has been proven false; the concrete reality which he thought to exist has vanished. He slowly fades from life, saying: 'He dado mi fruto y estoy de más' (IV. 1289). When his landlady, Javiera, observes that she sees no 'fruto', he replies: 'Es posible. Lo que se ve, señora doña Javiera, es la parte menos importante de lo que existe. Invisible es todo lo grande, toda ley, toda causa, todo elemento activo. Nuestros ojos, ¿qué son más que microscopios?' (IV. 1289). Even at the verge of death he indirectly maintains his superiority by implying that his 'fruto' is 'grande' and therefore invisible. Still human, Manso cannot accept that his view might lack validity. It is only after he returns to his 'mythical' abode and can view earthly life from a superhuman perspective that he sees clearly. He observes from the clouds (perhaps the only objective 'point of view'): ' ¡Dichoso estado y regiones dichosas estas en que puedo mirar a Irene, a mi hermano, a Peña, a doña Javiera, a Calígula, a Lica y demás desgraciadas figurillas con el mismo desdén con que el hombre maduro ve los juguetes que le entretuvieron cuando era niño!' (IV 1291). This is again a Cervantine reference; Don Quijote begins his discourse on the *Edad de Oro* with 'Dichosa edad y siglos dichosos aquéllos.'[10] With these last words of the novel Manso transcends his earthly prejudices fully, and now sees that what remains of his presence is 'poco, y no de lo mejor'. But considered from this ultimate perspective it is now all the same to him. The theater-of-the-world motif here connoted seems to suggest that truth cannot be found in reality, but only above or beyond it. With *El amigo Manso* the world is not only a stage, but also a novel, a construct of language.

With each refinement in his consideration of himself and of truth, Manso seemed to approximate the 'real' situation, without ever grasping it completely. His lesson is, to a certain extent, also our own in the process of reading this novel, and in applying it to life. A novel may tell us something about life that we would not have known before from mere experience: 'porque las lecciones de los libros muchas veces hacen más cierta experiencia de las cosas, que no la tienen los mismos que las han visto, a causa que el que lee con atención repara una y muchas veces en lo que va leyendo, y el que mira sin ella no repara en nada, y con esto excede la lección a la vista.'[11] 'But even reading does not presume absolute knowledge. The 'creation' of *El amigo Manso* ruptures the novel's illusion of realism, and its narrator destroys our ability to identify a single voice of truth. As Nancy Newton has commented, '*El amigo Manso* is structured on and gives evidence of the Galdosian disbelief in an absolute truth.' She concludes her study by saying: 'The wild multiples of reality – "sus maravillosas combinaciones" – cannot be tamed or harnessed by observation, by analysis, by metaphor, or any other intellectual construct. Such is the lesson that Máximo Manso, the intellectual construct of Galdós, communicates to us.'[12] It is a lesson about the function of point of view in fiction as well as in 'reality', which perhaps are one.

José María Bueno de Guzmán of *Lo prohibido* is another narrator–protagonist, in this case of a work which constitutes his 'autobiography'. As his name suggests, his narrative contains various picaresque elements. Sherman Eoff has observed that *Lo prohibido* provides 'a study in psychology and morality' through a revival of the picaresque genre, although not necessarily its modes of narrating events. While it is easy to appreciate that 'the view of personality in its relationship to environment' in *Lo prohibido* is similar to that of *Guzmán de Alfarache* in some particularly significant ways,[13] it is also possible to discern some important parallels in their modes of narration. Indeed, *Lo prohibido* reflects the narrative style of the *Guzmán* in many ways, the most important of which is that José María, like Guzmán de Alfarache, is supposedly relating his past life from a point of conversion and maturity. As in the *Guzmán*, this pretense, along with that of the autobiographical form itself, is never fully abandoned.[14] In *Lo prohibido* the questions of objectivity and point of view are posed again, and the conventions eventually undermined, although in a different manner from that in *El amigo Manso*.

José María's dual position as autobiographer and protagonist in his story (in which he ironically denies being the hero)[15] misleads the reader; he claims to be able to, but cannot, distance himself from the events of his own life. Since José María is the mediating agent between his life story and the reader, the reader must continually differentiate between a character and a narrator who are one and the same. The reader is forced into a conflict between a conventional tendency to sympathize with the protagonist (which the narrator encourages) and the detachment required for a critical understanding of the novel. We are denied any other perspective on José María than his own, since the other characters seldom have the opportunity to convey their observations of him directly to us through dialogue. Only the criticisms of José María by Camila are given to the reader at any length. The narrator continually excuses his past behavior with rationalizations, even when he seems to reproach himself for having seduced and corrupted two of his cousins and attempted to do the same with the third, Camila. On the other hand, José María's judgments about the other characters are quite harsh. He either overtly criticizes them, or mitigates their virtues by indirectly asserting his own superiority. When he praises Eloísa's discriminating taste and judgment, for example, he implicitly establishes his own capacity to evaluate her judgments. José María seems to deprecate himself, but by telling us that Eloísa consults him and that he recognizes her 'buen gusto', he returns the praise of her to him:

En repararlo modernizarlo [el edificio] ponía mi prima sus cinco sentidos, con aquella habilidad organizadora, aquel altísimo ingenio suntuario y artístico que la distinguía. Diariamente se asesoraba de mí sobre el color de una alfombra... ¡Ella, que era la propia musa del Buen Gusto, si me es permitido decirlo así, consultaba conmigo, el más lego de los hombres en estas materias, y que no sabía sino lo que ella me había enseñado! Pero, en fin, como Dios me daba a entender, yo la aconsejaba. (IV. 1695)

In another passage he examines Raimundo's intellectual abilities and also praises himself:

llegué a comprender que mi primo, dotado de aptitudes tan varias, no habría sido jamás poeta eminente, ni pintor de nota, ni músico, ni orador, ni cómico, ni crítico, aunque se dedicara exclusivamente a alguna de estas artes, porque carecía de fondo propio, de fuerza íntima, de esa impulsión moral, que es tan indispensable para los actos de creación artística como para las obras de la voluntad. (IV. 1690)

At the same time as he shows himself capable of defining Raimundo's failings, José María implicitly presumes his own moral and intellectual superiority to his cousin. The fact that he is writing a book indicates that he believes himself to be in possession of the 'fondo propio' so indispensable to artistic creation and acts of will. Yet José María's narration is wholly and subtly inverted as he reveals his own lack of moral character. According to his criteria, then, José María was incapable of writing *Lo prohibido*. The ambiguous ending of the novel reinforces this parodoxical and intensely ironical implication.

José María describes the other characters' inner motives according to his own prejudices, a procedure which constantly works to his advantage. Nonetheless, his generalizations offer ironic clues to their reliability and to that of the entire narration. José María often moves from a character's statements to a subjective conclusion based not on the words presented directly to the reader, nor even on those José María reports he heard, but on what he surmises the character thought. José María's observations often involve plays on words which undermine his point of view and sometimes ironically describe him. In one instance he relates some of his uncle's history of the family's neurotic afflictions, and employs the free indirect style which further complicates and confuses the narrative voices.[16] Then he summarizes the account and draws his own conclusions about what his uncle 'really' meant:

Al llegar aquí, la facundia de aquel gran hablador, engolosinada por la sangre de uno de sus yernos, a quien acababa de morder, la emprendió con los tres a un tiempo, dejándolos al fin bastante magullados. Hizo luego de mí, sin venir a cuento, elogios que me avergonzaron. Yo era, según él, un hombre como se ven pocos en el mundo, por las dotes físicas y por las morales. De todo este panegírico saqué otra vez en limpio, leyendo en la intención y en el desconsuelo de mi tío, que éste habría deseado que sus tres hijas fuesen una sola, y que esta hija única suya hubiera sido mi mujer. (IV. 1680)

His egotistical self-esteem is apparently tempered by the mediation of 'según él'. 'Leyendo en la intención' is a subjective conclusion as well as an ironic use of the verb *leer*. In another example, José María's judgment of his uncle Rafael is more directly self-descriptive and ironic: 'Parecíame algo fantástico lo que me contaba aquel hablador sempiterno, que, por lucir el ingenio, era capaz de alimentar su facundia con materiales de invención. —Usted hubiera sido un gran novelador —le dije' (IV. 1677). The conclusions which José María reaches about his uncle's (and other's) estimation of himself issue precisely from his own imagination. His words serve to ingratiate him with the reader, and to extend his novel and illustrate his *ingenio*. José María here indirectly describes his own role as a novelist who invents in order to reveal his *ingenio*.

Arthur Terry has written that José María's subjective views are countered, especially in Part II, by situations in which we see the other characters and can thus compare his opinions to our own observations. Indeed, José María becomes more reliable in the second part of the novel, and presents himself in compromising situations. At the same time, however, the veracity of the whole story is undermined; ironic allusions to the historicity of the narration become frequent, recalling *Don Quijote* and thus the novel's own fictionality. José María refers to himself in chapter I as 'el narrador de estos verídicos sucesos' (IV. 1774); and the title of chapter II is 'Sigo narrando cosas que vienen muy a cuento con esta verdadera historia.' These references, which paradoxically imply the work's fictionality and unreliability, culminate in the final chapter. José María is injured in an accident precipitated by his repeated attempts to seduce Camila. Now paralyzed, he is finishing his *Memorias*, transcribing them with the aid of Ido de Sagrario, the slightly mad writer of *folletines* who, he says, 'con sólo mirarme adivinábame los pensamientos' (IV. 1888). Ido wishes to add a few passages to the autobiography, but José María affirms and re-affirms that 'nada hay aquí que no sea escrupuloso traslado de la verdad. La única reforma que consentí fue variar los nombres de todas las personas que menciono, empezando por el mío; variación que realizamos con pena, pues me gustaría llevar la sinceridad a sus últimos límites' (IV. 1888). He states that his

prosaicas aventuras. . .[son]. . .sucesos que en nada se diferencian de los que llenan y constituyen la vida de otros hombres, y no aspiran a producir más efectos que los que la emisión fácil y sincera de la verdad produce, sin propósito de mover el ánimo del lector con rebuscados espantos, sorpresas y burladeros de pensamientos y de frase, haciendo que las cosas parezcan de un modo y luego resulten de otro.

Y no me habría sido difícil, sobre todo contando con la experta mano de mi inteligente pendolista, alterar la verdad dentro de lo verosímil en beneficio del interés. (IV. 1888)

This reiterated sincerity is rendered suspect by its very repetition and by self-reflective phrases such as 'prosaicas aventuras trasladas de la verdad' and 'la verdad dentro de lo verosímil'. His affirmation that 'me gustaría llevar la sinceridad a sus últimos límites' is a contrary-to-fact statement which applies to the whole narration, not just to the names of the characters. Indeed, it does seem that things appear 'de un modo y luego resultan de otro', and the reader *is* surprised and fooled. His narration is no more sincere than the virtuous and paternal consideration of Camila which he professes after his accident. José María's friend tell him that in his dreams – the realm of ultimate subjectivity – he speaks of Camila as his wife and of her child as his. Similarly, we have seen in the narration that José María cannot relate events objectively because he sees them only from his own perspective.

The novel ends with a final twist in this mediated presentation of the events to the reader. José María entrusts his manuscript to a friend of his and of Ido:

De acuerdo con Ido, remití el manuscrito, puesto ya en limpio y con los nombres bien disimulados, a un amigo suyo y mío que se ocupa de estas cosas, y aun vive de ellas, para que lo viese y examinara, disponiendo su publicación si conceptuaba digno del público mi mamotreto. . .Hoy ha venido el tal a verme; hablamos; le invito a escribir la historia de la *Prójima*, de la cual yo no he hecho más que el prólogo. . .Después de mi muerte puede darse mi amigo toda la prisa que quiera para sacarlas en letras de molde, y así la publicación del libro será la fúnebre esquela que vaya diciendo por el mundo a cuantos quieran saberlo que ya el infeli-císimo autor de estas confesiones habrá dejado de padecer. (IV. 1890)

Even at the point of death José María affirms his egocentricity with a back-handed compliment to himself: the fact that we are reading his 'mamotreto' indicates that his author friend (the ironic 'el tal') did conceive it as worthy of publication. Terry believes that José María's illness has stripped him of all self-esteem (p. 70), but even in the end there remains a shred of his subtle self-praise. The fictionality of these *Memorias* is confirmed by his attempts to assert their historicity, just as we have seen in Galdós' other works. Even the supposed publishing author becomes fictional through his incorporation in the narrative.

The conventional assumption that the narrator mediates the novel-istic events to the reader can thus be ironically undermined in various ways. If the narrator is misleading, ignorant, deceiving or deceived, the reader also may incur these limitations. The narrator can create irony through such devices as the free indirect style and explicit claims of truth and history. The 'voice of reading' may serve overt irony at any level, in addition to fostering that implicit irony which springs from our conventional interpretation of such a voice as more truthful, or at least as less fictional (and hence less a mere artifice of language), than the other parts of the novel. The narrator always remains, how-ever, another linguistic construct, another code of the fiction to which we lend a certain authority and autonomy. Its foundation remains language; whether the language appears as that of the characters' desires or of a narrator's insights, it ultimately constitutes a single and fictional text. Still, we often come to believe that language represents reality, or even replaces it when we forget its fictional essence. A character's or narrator's appeal to truth and objectivity masks another 'truth' which is just as valid, just as one reader's interpretation may be as valid as that of the next. In any novel, one reader's 'realism' may be another's 'romanticism'. Hayden White has observed that 'Irony thus represents a stage of consciousness in which the problematical nature of language itself has become recognized. It points to the poten-tial foolishness of all linguistic characterizations of reality as much as to the absurdity of the beliefs it parodies.'[17] *La incógnita* epitomizes this auto-deixis of language's intrinsic irony. It reveals its own ironic nature in the novel's act of pointing to society's irony. It is an epistolary novel, a form which, *par excellence*, invokes the autonomy of written language; its subject is reality, which we learn is merely opinion.

La incógnita (1888–9) is usually read together with the dialogue novel, *Realidad* (1889),[18] yet it is completely self-sufficient and continually manifests (as its title indicates) the various levels of the unknown, instead of the reality which its 'author' claims. The events of the story, ostensibly an adulterous love affair and the mysterious death of Federico Viera, seem more removed from us than those of the other novels analyzed because of the epistolary form employed. The letters of Manuel Infante to Equis X of Orbajosa expose Infante's weaknesses and the problems of perception he displays, rather than the depths of his friends' personalities which he claims to reveal. We see little of these other characters directly, since Infante reproduces their dialogues out of context. Like all aspects of the letters, these are colored by the intense subjectivity which Infante repeatedly calls the purest objectivity. His observations, though, are nothing more than opinions; and opinion, Tierno Galván has observed, hides a lack of substance.[19]

As in the other novels, various devices, such as self-contradiction, serve to reveal the irony of his objectivity. In Letter ii, for example, Infante describes the first of the characters that we meet, his *padrino*, Don Carlos Cisneros. He writes about his art collection, and then admits:

Y aquí ¡oh ínclito Equis!, mi sinceridad me hace soltar una herejía, que de seguro leerás con indignación...*Me cargan las antigüedades*...Es que no lo entiendo, y tengo la franqueza de decirlo, mientras que otros, sin entenderlo más que yo, fingen extasiarse delante de cualquier roñoso cachivache o de un trapo descolorido y mugriento. Excuso decirte que me guardaré muy bien de decir esto al amigo don Carlos. (v. 690)

Infante condemns in others the hypocrisy which he displays in public too. In other cases, Infante states 'facts' about others, only to eventually change them after he discovers another 'fact' which he later modifies in turn. Thus he reports the honor or dishonor of Augusta, the saintliness or madness of her husband Orozco, and whether or not Viera is her lover. Yet his 'facts' are only opinions, often completely mistaken. Federico Viera swears to Infante that he is not Augusta's lover (though we later discover he is), and Infante believes him because 'me lo juró en un tono tal de sinceridad, que no es posible creer que representara una comedia' (v. 738). Infante manifests the limitations of his ability to observe himself and others, rather than his incisive powers of insight. His affirmation of his belief in Viera subverts sincerity, and the criterion to which Infante appeals is the same as that which he proposes to Equis in support of the value of his observations: 'Sólo con la seguridad de que humanos ojos, fuera de los tuyos de ratón, no han de ver el contenido de estas cartas, puedo ser, como me propongo, absolutamente sincero al escribirlas' (v. 687). These words begin the novel with an ironic twist since we, of course, are also reading the letters. Like Infante, we may think that sincerely expressed words signify the truth, but they only truly signify themselves.

The narration of the epistolary novel in the first person by the exemplary writer continually displays its subjectivity. The text bespeaks the 'I' through its peculiarly 'discursive' character, through the total mediation of events by the letter-writer, and through the story of one man's investigations into a love triangle which he hopes to penetrate. At each of these levels the text reveals the inability of the subject to capture the object: Infante never solves the mystery of Federico and Augusta, nor does he ever win Augusta's love for himself. The reader cannot solve the intrigue either; even the text's miraculous metamorphosis into the manuscript of *Realidad* (a gesture which recalls the origin of 'El curioso impertinente' in *Don Quijote*) does not totally reveal *La incógnita*. *Realidad* is *La incógnita*; we are told in the last letter, the only one which Equis writes to Infante, that they have the same hand-writing: 'Pues anteayer se me antojó releerlas [las cartas]. Abro mi arca y... ¡puff! Sin juramento me puedes creer que salía de allí un olor de mil demonios. Echo mano al paquete, y me lo encuentro transformado en el drama o novela dialogada, *de tu puño y letra* (v. 787). This equation of *La incógnita* and *Realidad* illustrates the ultimate mystery of reality itself; neither the characters nor the reader is permitted to understand the situation thoroughly, even in *Realidad*. As this metamorphosis indicates, moreover, language, and especially the written, fails to express reality, and instead becomes it.

Infante's observations are only opinions, but opinion forms what we effectively accept as reality, whether in the novel or in the world around us. Just like Infante as he reads his text, we are forced by the nature of *La incógnita* (which parodies at one level the *novela policíaca* and thus demands even more interpretation) to form our opinions about the events, Infante, and the meaning of the novel. Our reading possesses a specular relationship with the movement of the story, as we, like Infante, strive to interpret it. Infante epitomizes the reading processes of expectation and retrospection (discussed by Iser) in his 'reading' of his novelistic society; it is the same process which we pursue when we read our own and the novel's society. Infante's opinions, like

our own, are constantly being modified as our judgments are elabor-
ated.[20] Again and again we see in this novel that whatever we accept
as a correct interpretation can be subverted in some way so that it
displays another level of meaning opposed to the one just formed.
Literary interpretation is just as much an opinion (although, one hopes,
an 'informed' one) as is Infante's appraisal of his story.

With each letter it gradually becomes evident that Infante's process
of discovering reality is in fact an exposition of his imagination trans-
lated into written language; it does not enjoy any necessary correspondence with the novelistic situation, which exists, of course, only in
our imagination since there is nothing beyond Infante's words. As he
describes his cousin Augusta, he comments: 'empiezo por decirte que
Augusta no me pareció, la primera vez que la vi, tan hermosa como yo
me la representaba. No puedo olvidar que nunca me diste una opinión
terminante sobre ella...Sobre si es o no hermosa, ya cabe mayor
variedad de opiniones' (v. 692). Before he even knew her, Infante
formed an imaginary vision – or opinion – of her beauty, and after
seeing her he describes her in what he believes are accurate terms.
Because of their metaphoric quality, these are doubly imaginary:
'tiene mi prima unos ojos negros que te marean si fijamente te miran;
ojos que llevan en sí el vértigo de las alturas y el misterio de las pro-
fundidades – aguántate esa imagen–, ojos que...no sigo por temor a
mi retórica y a tus guasitas' (v. 692). He recognizes his own rhetoric,
but not its effect, since he believes his words and opinions are accurate.
He is enchanted by the very eyes that he believes he is describing so
objectively, at the same time as he is falling in love with her. In other
letters Infante seems to recognize his debt to rhetoric, art, and the
novel even more overtly, yet he does not apply this to an evaluation
of his own observations and their fictional value. The distance between the 'physical' Augusta and Infante's imaginary representation
of her develops into an irreconcilable opposition that even Infante
sees:

hace días que me encuentro sorprendido con invencible tendencia a pensar
en ella, a figurármela delante de mí...a suponer y anticiparme las
[palabras] que me ha de decir la primera vez que nos veamos. Al propio
tiempo, nace en mi espíritu una admiración irreflexiva hacia ella, y me
sorprendo a mí mismo en la tarea ideal de adornarla con las más excelentes cualidades que jamás embellecieron a criatura alguna. De aquí nace
mi mayor pena, pues precisamente las cualidades que le atribuyo ponen
una barrera moral entre ella y yo. Para imaginar que esta aspiración mía
[de ser su amante], incierta y tímida, pueda satisfacerse alguna vez, tengo

que destruir mi propia obra, y exonerar a la señora de mis pensamientos, quitándole aquellas mismas perfecciones que le supuse. (v. 700–1)

Infante is attracted to Augusta because he imagines her as beautiful and pure; however, this image of her causes him to attempt to seduce her, an act which would destroy his imaginary lover, and thus his desire. The two Augustas whom Infante envisions and constantly fluctuates between are both equally imaginary. He denies Equis' assertion that Augusta is dishonorable:

La opinión que en tu carta me indicas respecto a mi prima no me parece ajustada a la verdad...Reconozco, señor maestro, que varío la tocata con demasiada frecuencia. Es que yo no me aferro a las opiniones, ni tengo la estúpida vanidad de la consecuencia del juicio. Observo lealmente, rectifico cuando hay que rectificar, quito y pongo lo que me manda quitar y poner la realidad, descubriéndose por grados, y persigo la verdad objetiva, sacrificándole la subjetiva, que suele ser un falso ídolo fabricado por nuestro pensamiento para adorarse en efigie. (v. 719)

Not only does Infante not recognize his own opinion as such, but he soon changes it again after hearing others' opinions of Augusta. His comment that the subjective truth is a false idol fabricated by our thought to adorn itself in effigy describes precisely what he himself does when he calls his subjectivity the most calculating objectivity.

Opinion is the essence of observation, truth, and reality; it informs the language of the novel and of the individual portraits it contains. 'Esta opinión, o, si quieres, semblanza o retrato, llevará el carácter de provisional, por no encontrarme en posesión de todos los datos para darla por definitiva' (v. 741). Infante makes this remark about Orozco, but the statement can be applied to the other levels of the novel as well. Infante's analysis and description of the characters and events are the same as the reader's appreciation of them. We are never given enough data to solve the novelistic mystery, nor can we form more than an opinion, however educated, about the meaning of the novel. But Infante does not see this about himself. While discussing the first murder in the novel (a foreshadowing of Viera's) he comments:

Es la conversación de moda en todos los círculos de Madrid, y personas muy formales ven en esto una intriga honda...
Las dos opiniones, que claramente se marcan ya, han dado origen a dos bandos encarnizados, en cada uno de los cuales la imaginación de esta raza fabrica toda clase de extravagancias novelescas. Y no es el vulgo el que más fecundidad muestra y más apetito de versiones maravillosas y pesimistas, pues la gente de cultura no le va en zaga. (v. 740)

Although Infante labels the speculations of others about this intrigue 'imaginary', he nonetheless offers a few of his own; this reflects the unconsciously subjective – not objective – speculation which pervades his letters. Even more, it recalls the imaginative process by which we ourselves label the novel a fiction, while ignoring the fictions of ourselves and our society.

As the story progresses it becomes more obvious – even to Infante, in some ways – that opinion or language creates and replaces the effective world. Federico Viera's poor but aristocratic sister marries a 'commoner', and Infante explains that 'Ahí tienes a la señora realidad haciendo muy calladita lo que escribís en vuestros libros y otros dicen en sus discursos. Yo te pregunto: ¿precede la idea al hecho, o el hecho a la idea? Pero dejémonos de averiguaciones y vete enterando de la realidad' (v. 749). Like opinion or spoken language, literature or written language forms and becomes reality. But Infante ignores his own insight and turns immediately to a discussion of Augusta's mysterious lover, an affair which he now considers 'realidad', but which he had appraised as 'una bien ensayada comedia para envolverme y confundirme' (v. 748). Infante describes Viera's death from a gunshot, an apparent suicide, with a (doubly) literary translation that recalls our constant characterization (if not perception) of events in literary terms: 'La sorpresa, el pavor de esta misteriosa tragedia' (v. 751). He and the other characters then abandon their discussion of the old 'drama' for the more recent one: 'Otra cosa reparé, y es que aquella noche no se habló de crimen. Bastante teníamos con aquella realidad fresca y que nos tocaba tan de cerca. Las emociones jurídicas del otro drama, antiguo ya y manoseado a fuerza de representaciones, perdían su novelesco interés' (v. 754). Infante, like them, indulges in this imaginative, literarily conditioned discussion. But he fails, as always, to recognize this literariness in his own words, and continues to offer his opinions about those of others:

Fácilmente comprenderás que un asunto de tal naturaleza...ha de excitar vivamente la chismografía de la raza más chismográfica del mundo; raza dotada de fecundidad prodigiosa para poner variantes a los hechos y adornarlos hasta que no los conoce la madre que los parió; raza esencialmente artista y plasmadora, que crea casos y caracteres, formando una realidad verosímil dentro y encima de la realidad auténtica. Ante un suceso de gran resonancia, todo español se cree humillado si no da sobre él su opinión firme, tanto mejor cuanto más distinta de los demás. Oí, como puedes figurarte, explicaciones razonables; otras, novelescas, aunque dotadas de esa verosimilitud propia de las obras de imaginación escritas con talento... Todo lo oí con paciencia y atención, pues hasta los mayores desatinos deben, en casos tales, oírse y sopesarse para obtener la verdad. (v. 762)

This passage displays the ironic self-interpretation which occurs throughout the novel, and includes the global characterization of *La incógnita* itself, which is likened to 'otras, novelescas, aunque dotadas de esa verosimilitud propia de las obras de imaginación escritas con talento'. The novel is also a category of the social ambience from which it springs: 'como vivimos en plena atmósfera novelesca' (v. 763). Indeed, the novel indicates that there is no independent truth or reality; all is novel, opinion, and words, as Cisneros advises Infante:

—La santa verdad, hijo de mi alma, no la encontrarás nunca, si no bajas tras ella al infierno de las conciencias, y esto es imposible. Conténtate con la verdad relativa y aparente, una verdad fundada en el honor, y que sacaremos, con auxilio de la ley, de entre las malicias del vulgo. El honor y las formas sociales nos imponen esa verdad, y a ella nos atenemos. (v. 765)

The reader is advised that all social norms, including Cisneros' concept of honor, form a linguistic code which sustains a whole moral and ethical literature (more fully scrutinized in *Realidad*) ultimately capable of legitimizing Viera's suicide.

Words create reality, or rather they supplant it by their super-imposition upon a reality which can never be known, if it exists at all. Words call attention to themselves and mask, rather than illuminate, what they appear to describe. Our perception becomes more distorted the further it is mediated. Language itself, more than any personified 'narrator', is the narrator of irony. This is why Infante is always misled; he accepts the words of others instead of examining their acts. This process pervades perceptions of all types:

El coche había recorrido la calle Ancha, y atravesaba Chamberí para bajar a la Castellana por las casas de Indo. Densa niebla luminosa y blanca se aplanaba sobre Madrid. No se veían las casas ni los árboles. Las luces de gas, desvaneciéndose en la claridad lechosa, formaban discos, en algunos puntos teñidos de un viso rosado, en otros de verde. Augusta y yo observamos aquel fenómeno, y alguna observación hicimos acerca de él; pero en realidad lo que decíamos era un pretexto para ocultar nuestra turbación. No era yo sólo el intranquilo y preocupado; ella también lo estaba. (v. 737–8)

This fogging, distorting effect is an image of Infante's opinions. Gimeno Casalduero observes of the commonplace which opinion constitutes: 'Aparece como una cortina de humo que oculta una realidad,

o mejor, una vacuidad.'[21] Infante persuades only himself, rather than
Augusta, in his final rhetorical declaration of love to her; even though
he now imagines her to be dishonored and perhaps a murderess, he
loves her all the more:

Y mira tú qué cosa tan rara: piensa en el enlace misterioso de las palabras
con los afectos en esta arrastrada vida humana, tan fecunda que cuantas
más cosas peregrinas ve uno en ella, más le quedan por ver. Pues empecé
a dirigirle aquellas frases amorosas que te he copiado, como quien emplea
un argumento capcioso; se las dije, persuadido de que no decía la verdad,
y al concluir, sorprendíme de ver que mi corazón respondía a todas aquellas retóricas con un sentimiento afirmativo. (v. 779–80)

Language supersedes and becomes reality. This phenomenon allows us
to 'suspend our disbelief' when reading novels.

The epistolary form, because it appears more 'written' than other
types of novels, offers an especially apt means for displaying language's
consciousness of its intrinsic irony. Galdós uses this form in other works
to achieve the same effect, though *La incógnita* is his only fully
epistolary novel in the *serie contemporánea*. In *Tristana*, for example,
Tristana's letters to Horacio reveal to the reader that her ideal of love
and of a lover ultimately efface his material existence for her. She writes
at one point: 'Mi señor, ¿cómo eres? Mientras más te adoro, más
olvido tu fisonomía; pero te invento otra a mi gusto, según mis ideas,
según las perfecciones de que quiero ver adornada tu sublime persona'
(v. 1591). In the course of their correspondence Tristana moves further
and further from any realistic conception of Horacio and their relationship, which was from the beginning formed largely from literary
commonplaces.[22] When Horacio finally returns, she at first fails to
recognize him and they eventually learn that they no longer have anything in common.

By means of the epistolary form, Galdós' novels demonstrate how
language reveals that the notion of objective reality is vacuous. Numerous other devices do this too: for example the extended use of *frases
hechas* and *lugares comunes* illustrates the phenomenon, discussed by
Tierno Galván and Gimeno Casalduero, of a ritualized and thoughtless
social expression.[23] Galdós attributes these modes of expression to
characters whose ironic sense is obvious, as well as to the narrator;
both gestures further the irony of the narration, and, more subtly, of
the reader. By accepting these commonplace expressions as meaningful,
the reader responds to them in the same way as do the characters.
These commonplaces are only a social convention, a formulaic void

with no fixed meaning. Language ultimately masks this vacuity, because reality cannot be known. Language is a means of approaching it, but it remains elusive, nonetheless.

So far this chapter has examined the modes of narration, their corresponding 'points of view', and the ways in which they structure the novelistic ironies. The conventional consideration of a mediation between characters and reader again must be re-evaluated in the dialogue novel, however. Even the illusion of a mediator has nearly vanished here, yet the irony remains. Iser has offered these observations (p. 160) about the dialogue novel:

in the absence of authorial explanation and definitive characterization, the reader is forced to make his own diagnosis. At the same time, however, by giving such an interpretation, he is automatically excluding other possibilities...The dialogue by its very nature defies any standardized interpretation, and yet the reader is always inclined to try and standardize, comparing the fictitious characters with his own experience and attempting to bring them into line with his own familiar world.

This drive to interpret, or naturalize, the characters' words often precipitates the ironic subversion of such an interpretation. It requires a retrospective re-evaluation of previous analyses as well as the elaboration of expectations consistent with the new novelistic material and its significance according to standards of the reader's world.[24] The reader continually builds his own ironies by negating his previous determinations of the novel's true meaning. The dialogue novel in particular demonstrates how this ironic process is intrinsic to reading itself, and does not require a narrator to achieve it.

With *Realidad* Galdós applies to an extreme the technique which already formed portions of previous novels: *La desheredada, El doctor Centeno, Tormento,* and *La de Bringas.* According to the Prologue of *El abuelo* (1897), another dialogue novel, the use of dialogue without narrative commentary presents a mixture of novel and drama in the manner of *La Celestina.* Such a form cuts across distinctions of genre, about which Galdós notes: 'como en todo lo que pertenece al reino infinito del Arte, lo más prudente es huir de los encasillados y de las clasificaciones catalogales de géneros y formas' (VI. 11). Galdós' intention, he tells us, is to allow the characters to stand out in relief, to reveal themselves without any apparent mediation. Iser notes that this form places the reader so close to the characters that he almost participates with them; while it establishes multiple perspectives on the novel, the

reader's is no longer privileged (see Iser, pp. 154ff. and 237ff.). There
is no narrator to qualify the characters' words, desires or acts, as there
was with Isidora Rufete, for example, who was finally said to be
engañada. Nor is there any foreshadowing or retrospection implied by
the narrator which might tell us more than what is 'present' in the
text. We have no temporal distance from the characters in a continuous
dialogue, Iser maintains (p. 235), although this distance is only a
convention or illusion in other types of novels anyway. We are only
given the characters' words, with no pretense of a 'voice of truth'; the
'voice of reading' is thus ours alone. We are privileged over the
characters only to the degree that we can see them all as they see each
other and can be 'present' in scenes where some of them are not. But
because we alone create the voice of reading, we alone deceive ourselves.

In *Realidad*, we must decide who is mad and who sane, who is right
and who wrong; neither this novel nor any of the dialogue novels gives
any final answer. Here there is a destruction of even the most rudi-
mentary conventions upon which we rely in order to justify and
rationalize those beliefs and decisions of ours which, because of irony,
are never absolute. Even multiple perspectives will not provide the one
true perspective, although they may seem more valid than the absolute
subjectivity of the letter-writer. Multiple perspectives, instead, force
the reader to question his own; the unpredictability of reality becomes
apparent in the unpredictability of the characters' words and their
implications. Iser has observed that the dialogue novel shifts the focus
of attention from the character's identity to his unpredictability and
thereby lessens, it might be added, our conventional tendency toward
'identification'. The character's appearance becomes less important –
characters are often not described in Galdós' dialogue novels – because
emphasis is placed on 'the wealth of implications...in every utterance'
(Iser, p. 157). Without such narrative conventions, the reader is forced
to pursue a more sophisticated reading process, and is less likely to fall
victim to the naive ironies which accompany identification.

The reader realizes that irony exists at all levels in *Realidad*, from
the characters' contradictory opinions about themselves and others to
the final dilemma of the novel. There the reader is faced with two
possible interpretations, both of which are equally incompatible with
his social conscience; the written ultimately offers no clue for resolving
this extra-textual dilemma. Iser proposes (p. 161) that

The reader himself must strive to make sense of their [the characters'] inconsistencies, but instead of discovering the motives for their conduct, he will merely find that the concrete statements he has read are over-shadowed by the statements that have not been written. The [written] spoken word, as a manifestation of the pragmatic self, proves to be nothing but a particle of subjectivity, its incompleteness made abundantly clear by the fact that no sooner has it been uttered than it is swamped by its own unformulated implications. In this accentuation of the unwritten lies the dynamism of the dialogue, and if the characters seem strangely unaffected by a confrontation with these implications, the reader will be that much more aware not only of their blindness but also of the irrelevance of their actual conduct [or of the plot].

The unwritten takes place in the reader's mind, but ultimately offers no more sense than the words spoken by the characters. In *Realidad*, the oppositions made by the characters between relatives and absolutes, words and ideals, and fiction and reality dissolve and their terms be-come indistinguishable.

The 'action' of *Realidad* corresponds to the period between Letters xxiv and xxxi of *La incógnita*. Gonzalo Sobejano has observed that *La incógnita* concerns the surface of reality while *Realidad* analyzes interior reality because its characters are presented in their subjective (chiefly through soliloquy) as well as their objective moments.[25] This characterization of the two works' relationship may not be entirely acceptable; although we are told in *Realidad* that Federico Viera was indeed Augusta's lover and that his ideal of honor drove him to suicide, our knowledge extends no further. Augusta views both the code of honor which forced Viera to his death and Orozco's idealized state of moral perfection as forms of madness. She sees each of them as repre-senting a lofty, conventional perspective which is nonetheless irrational. There is, however, no narrator to qualify Augusta's judgment, which is a conventionally rational and socially acceptable attitude toward madness, but expressed by an adulteress. If the reader sympathizes with the position of either Orozco and Viera or Augusta, he must re-evaluate some of his own standards regarding the nature of honor, sanity and morality; these labels also contain their fictions. This dilemma serves to distance the reader from the characters whose soliloquies had rendered them so close to him. Even more, it recalls the distance which we should always maintain from the novel, and the insuperable distance which always separates us from absolute know-ledge of reality.

The conviction that there can be no absolutes, that all is relative, constantly informs this novel, beginning with the title. *Realidad*, as we have seen already, is forever *la incógnita*. Moreover, it is ironic that such a title, besides introducing the dialogue novel which claims to be so objective, should be applied to the utterly fantastic and subjective. Clarín criticized Galdós' use of a dramatic form for treating a psychological subject.[26] But this seems to be simply one more irony; the form which is seemingly most objective is used to analyze a most subjective material. Among the three major characters, Orozco constructs ideal standards unrelated to real circumstances (and finally sees Viera's ghost). Viera considers Orozco's goodness unreal (and confesses to him in hallucinations). Augusta cannot distinguish her dreams from her experiences when awake. The fantastic concepts which Viera and Orozco have of each other become so vivid that they assume physical form in Viera's hallucinations and Orozco's supernatural encounter; these visions become more important to them than any other experience. Augusta is so tormented by the consciousness of her fault that her recollection of the scene of Viera's death and her somnambulate confession to her husband Orozco are indistinguishable to her from her conscious actions. For all three characters, their ideals or fears become their realities, and for Viera and Orozco, ultimately, their only reality. All three are motivated by conventional codes – of honor, morality, and love – which they believe to be absolute. These codes may be literary, yet they are sufficient; the aristocratic society of the novel is based on cultural and ethical systems which have no necessary relationship to the 'real' world.

Augusta's love for Viera is a product of her perspective on life; she is always searching for the stylized and the romanticized as when she says to him: 'Es que sin darme cuenta de ello, todo lo vulgar me parece falso, tan alta idea tengo de la realidad...como artista; ni más ni menos' (v. 800). Her desire to compare life with art – or to exchange them – is so overpowering that she allows herself to be directed by her fictions, without realizing it. The distinctions which she believes that she makes between the two become inverted. During an amorous interlude with Viera, Augusta tries to convince him to accept Orozco's money in order to live decently; she rationalizes to him: 'Es que me transformo, es que aspiro a fundir la ilusión con la razón, a hacerte feliz en todos los terrenos, a establecer tu vida junto a la mía, en condiciones de estabilidad' (v. 826). Her idea of *razón* is just as illusory as her *ilusión* of love, because Viera does not really love her, but rather has seduced her as an adventure (v. 820). Viera reminds her that she is married; she replies:

Es cierto. Con esa idea me traes a la vida real. Iba yo por los espacios imaginarios, como las brujas que vuelan montadas en una escoba. Pero, en fin...es preciso nos volvamos muy prosaicos, muy caseros...

...Acábese el romanticismo y empiece la época positiva, positivista o como quieras llamarla. Es menester, amigo de mi alma, que nos pongamos en prosa. (v. 826)

Augusta's ideas are replete with literary clichés; her distinctions between 'ilusión' and 'razón', 'vida real' and 'espacios imaginarios', 'romanticismo' and 'la época positivista', and 'poesía' and 'prosa' are all equally contrived and impractical. Her concept of reality is totally idealized. Her love, which she swears is eternal, is founded on the conventions of literature; we learn that she is persuaded by words, not by her own sentiments, when she confesses to Orozco in a dream:

Ya, ya sé qué es lo primero que debo decir: cuándo empezó mi infidelidad y la razón de ella. ¿La razón de ella? ¡Yo qué sé! Esas cosas no tienen razón. Le traté algún tiempo, ya casada, sin sospechar que le quería con amor. No caí en la cuenta de que estaba prendada de él sino cuando me declaró que se había prendado de mí. Tres días de ansiedad y de lucha precedieron a uno memorable para mí...Le amé locamente, y cuando me fuí enterando de sus desgracias, de las cadenas ocultas que arrastra el pobrecito, le quise más, le adoré. (v. 808)

It was his language which inspired her sentiments and now forms her obsession, even in his death:

¡Verle morir así, sin que en su agonía tuviera para mí una palabra de ternura!...Recordarás que me dió un nombre ofensivo, ultrajante, el apodo de esa mujerzuela...

¿Por qué no me dijo una palabra cariñosa, que yo pudiera recordar después como consuelo? (v. 893)

When her maid reminds her that he asked for God's pardon, Augusta laments:

Eso es, perdón a Dios, y a mí que me partiera un rayo...Yo estoy muerta de pena y desconsuelo; de pena por él, porque le amé quizá más de lo que se merecía; desconsolada porque no le volveré a ver, porque murió queriéndome poco o nada, dejándome afligida y celosa...sí, celosa... ¡Si yo pudiera olvidar esta terrible pesadilla [de llamarme por otro nombre]! ...No, no hay tiempo bastante largo para borrar esto. (v. 893)

The last words Viera uttered, as well as those he did not, obsess Augusta more than his actual death.

The comments of other characters indicate that the illusions which drive Viera to the real act of suicide are based on a literary code of honor: ' ¡Ay, amigo mío...no echas de ver que ya han quedado muy atrás los tiempos calderonianos!' (v. 816); 'Este señorito fantasioso cree que estamos en tiempos como los de esas comedias en que salen las cómicas con manto, y los cómicos con aquellas espadas tan largas, y hablando en consonancia. ¡Válgate Dios con la quijotería!' (v. 816). A Calderonian code of honor and social order determines Viera's behavior: 'lo que aquí se llama el honor, una especie de cédula o cartilla, sin la cual no se puede vivir' (v. 877). Augusta labels as social demand what Viera believes his honor dictates: ' ¡Fantasmón, esclavo de la letra y de la forma! Sacrificas tu felicidad y la mía al respeto social, a esa paparrucha del "qué dirán", a la opinión de cuatro estúpidos' (v. 883). As in *La incógnita*, 'opinión' is again criticized here. Augusta repeatedly condemns social conventions as absurd, but nonetheless plays her 'comedia' in front of her husband and friends after Viera's death (see p. 893, for example). Plays on words such as 'novela', 'comedia', 'arte', and 'pongamos en prosa' pervade the text and further ironize the theme of fiction versus reality with which this fiction called *Realidad* deals. Like Augusta, Orozco and Viera claim to reject social conventions, and call them false; yet they themselves are driven by equally fictional forces.

All the characters, like Infante, engage in opinionizing. After Viera's death, Villalonga and Malibrán discuss its possible cause. Villalonga warns Malibrán not to spread any malicious opinions about Augusta, but they still speculate about what occurred. Malibrán's opinion, Villalonga observes, is 'verosímil'. He replies in dramatic terms: 'Tan verosímil, que yo me represento la escena como si la estuviera viendo y eschuchara la voz de ambos personajes' (v. 889). They agree that they are right (which they are not) and the verisimilitude of their representation of the scene becomes reality for them. Even Orozco, who claims to have distanced himself completely from these social fictions, engages in them, and dwells in his own imaginary world where he thinks himself free to disdain 'este museo de la opinión' (v. 891). At the very end of the novel, when Orozco believes that he and Viera are embracing across eternity in the realm of 'el bien absoluto', his final words are still no more than opinion:

Oye lo que pienso de tu muerte...¡Ay! Por Dios, no te apoyes en mi pecho...Pues mi opinión es que moriste por estímulos del honor y de la conciencia; te arrancaste la vida porque se te hizo imposible colocada entre mi generosidad y mi deshonra. Has tenido flaquezas, has cometido faltas enormes; pero la estrella del bien resplandece en tu alma. Eres de los míos. Tu muerte es un signo de grandeza moral. Te admiro y quiero que seas mi amigo en esta región de paz en que nos encontramos. Abracémonos. (*Se abrazan.*) (v. 901)

By calling Viera a man after his own heart, Orozco accepts a code of honor which we know is literarily and socially conditioned. To the end, Orozco's 'grandeza moral' involves the most deeply ingrained social and literary conventions, which his imagination has converted into the most effective reality. This phenomenon is no different than the 'imágenes' and 'sombras' which the characters see without being able to distinguish them from physical persons. As Orozco notes, his ideas are so powerful that they can be converted into perceptible images: '[las ideas] se apoderan de mi mente con despótico empuje, y tal es su fuerza plasmadora, que no dudo puedan convertirse en imágenes perceptibles' (v. 899). (The word 'despótico', like the exclamation 'por Dios, no te apoyes en mi pecho' which Orozco utters upon embracing Viera's ghost, serve to undermine the sublime connotations which Orozco would lend to his ideal world.) When Viera sees Orozco's spirit before his death, he does not know if it is real: 'tengo mis dudas de si fue realidad o ficción de mi mente lo que vieron mis ojos y escucharon mis oídos' (v. 882). He concludes by deciding that the physical Orozco with whom he spoke in the theater was instead imaginary. Augusta calls the 'bien absoluto' which Orozco and Viera attain a 'locura'. For all of them, their imaginary life directs – or replaces, in the case of Viera and Orozco – their physical and social existence. But their new codes of behavior are just as artificial as those of society which they believe they are rejecting. Clarín criticized the rhetorical tenor which pervades the characters' soliloquies, saying (pp. 201–2) that it creates a 'saborcillo humorístico', inappropriate to 'los grandes momentos del conflicto moral' of Orozco and Viera. Yet the dependence of their exalted ideals upon cultural and social codes simply reaffirms the irony of their belief in the autonomy of their behavior and the certainty of their knowledge. This ironic humor and the events of the story offer the same tragicomedy as *Don Quijote*.

All these dualities – the humor and seriousness of both the soliloquy and its topic, the tragedy and comedy in the theme of *Realidad*, the novel's objective form and subjective material, and the *bien absoluto* and *locura* of Orozco – all these maintain the ironic relationships which this novel effects. There is no truth that can be wholly perceived as non-fictional, because irony is always present to reveal its fiction. There are no absolutes in morality or society, nor are there in reading. The voice of truth, like the narrator, is an illusion. We can never be sure that our reading is the correct one, because another interpretation always stands in opposition to it, just as *locura* stands to *bien absoluto*, or Don Quijote's *locura* to his *cordura*. This is especially well illustrated in the dialogue novel where the reader is forced to evaluate the narrative for himself without benefit of a guiding voice. An ambiguous ending further contributes to the over-all uncertainty of the reading process. The other dialogue novels also display this uncertain resolution which subverts conventional morality by impeding a conventionally moralistic reading. *La loca de la casa* (1892) ends with a reunion of Cruz, who seems to symbolize evil, with Victoria, who appears to be symbolic of purity and goodness. The last words of the story are Victoria's as she responds to Cruz, who demands that she confess that they cannot live without each other: 'Lo confieso, sí. Eres el mal, y si el mal no existiera, los buenos no sabríamos qué hacer...no podríamos vivir' (v. 1676). The ending of *El abuelo* also unites opposites: El Conde and his daughter-in-law's illegitimate daughter find that they love each other more than do he and his legitimate granddaughter. Don Pío asks, in the last words of the novel: 'El mal, ¿es el bien?'

The conclusions which the reader might provide for these and other novelistic dilemmas can always be made ironic by other, opposing conclusions; none of them can claim any existence more certain than the words which constitute them. These words fold back upon themselves in a continuous play of unlimited significations. The narrator of irony emerges from the narrator himself; the language of irony emerges from language itself. The text strives to encompass a representation – to establish limited significations – which always eludes it. The language of the text proffers a literary, rhetorical, and cultural surrogate for a reality which we assume it represents – yet never does – but which it may supersede.

4

The texture of irony

Torquemada en la hoguera is the shortest of the *Novelas contemporáneas*, and readily lends itself to a comprehensive analysis of its ironic intertextualities. The novella is a dense complex of ironic allusions which function from the level of a single word, to that of the act of reading. The elaboration of these ironies is achieved primarily through the presentation and subsequent subversion of recognized codes of meaning: cultural and literary motifs, themes, symbols, and conventions. Despite its brevity, the diversity and complexity of the codes which traverse *Torquemada en la hoguera* make an exhaustive study of the novella nearly impossible.[1] This chapter simply attempts to outline some of the principal ironic features at work, in order to suggest how they effect its portraits, settings, and narration, and thus contribute to the total ironic texture. A more or less syntagmatic analysis of the novella will parallel the process through which its complex of ironies offers itself for reading.

The evocation of historical and symbolic connotations begins with the title. The name Torquemada cannot be read without recalling the notorious Inquisitor. The image of the *hoguera* alludes to the *autos da fe*, reinforces the motif of the Inquisition, and also alludes to the symbolic hell of the protagonist's life. The first paragraph confirms and expands these connotations in its cumulating clauses:

> Voy a contar cómo fué al quemadero el inhumano que tantas vidas infelices consumió en llamas; que a unos les traspasó los hígados con un hierro candente; a otros les puso en cazuela bien mechados, y a los demás los achicharró por partes, a fuego lento, con rebuscada y metódica saña. Voy a contar cómo vino el fiero sayón a ser víctima; cómo los odios que provocó se le volvieron lástima, y las nubes de maldiciones arrojaron sobre él lluvia de piedad; caso patético, caso muy ejemplar, señores, digno de contarse para enseñanza de todos, aviso de condenados y escarmiento de inquisidores. (v. 906)

This initial paragraph contains important indications of how the ironies of the story are written and might be read. The self-conscious character of its language is apparent in the rhythmical diction and parallel syntax of the two sentences that compose it, each of which begins with the anaphoric 'Voy a contar'. These words invoke the dramatic posture of the *titiritero*, the manipulator *par excellence* who usually presents himself primarily as a moralist. The last third of the final sentence reaffirms this moralistic approach: 'caso patético, caso muy ejemplar, señores, digno de contarse para enseñanza de todos'. The apostrophe to 'señores' and the words 'ejemplar' and 'enseñanza' are overtly moralistic, and the preterite signals that the events occurred in the past. This places the narrator, and the reader whom he is privileging with foreknowledge of what is to happen, at a seemingly safe distance from this ferocious victim.

The brevity of the work, the moralistic tone, and the particular words 'ejemplar' and 'enseñanza' recall Cervantes and his *Novelas ejemplares*. The numerous allusions to 'historiadores inéditos' and other 'historical' references like this one which begins the second paragraph, continually confirm that Cervantes' work lies behind and within this story, as it does with so many of Galdós' novels. The first two lines of *La gitanilla* offer a perspective on the narrative and characters which is not unlike that of *Torquemada en la hoguera*: 'Parece que los gitanos y gitanas solamente nacieron en el mundo para ser ladrones...que no se quitan [las ganas de hurtar] sino con la muerte. Una, pues...crió una muchacha en nombre de nieta suya...a quien enseñó todas sus... trazas de hurtar.'[2] The story, of course, is not about the thievery of Preciosa, nor of the gypsies. These initial lines lead the reader to expect something which he will not necessarily encounter. The same is true in *Torquemada en la hoguera* where the reader is told that he will be reading a primarily moralistic and symbolic tale. But unlike the *Novelas ejemplares*, which claimed to fulfill the Horatian dictum of *deleitar y enseñar*, the first paragraph of *Torquemada en la hoguera* does not include the 'delightful' aspect of the story along with the 'instructive'. In fact, it becomes apparent that the reader will not be permitted to simply relax and enjoy the novella from a distance. He will be drawn into the text – a process already subtly begun by his implied complicity with the narrator – and, like the characters, will be manipulated and even ironized. The initial distance of the first paragraph and the partially compassionate tone distract the reader's attention, in order to dissimulate the ironic significance of the tale and its telling. This deception is displayed in the highly metaphoric language of the two opening sentences. The metaphors seem to place the entire story within the realm of the symbolic, not the *cotidiano*. But this symbolic code, like the moralistic and literary, will soon be subverted in the process of affirmation and negation which continually affects the work.

The key to seeing these other, subversive meanings in the novella is found in one word, 'contar'. It is used three times in the paragraph, and will be repeated endlessly in the text; it means both 'to count' and 'to recount'. It is the *logos* in which the language of the money-lender and that of the narrator come together. 'Contar' articulates a symbolic code in the purest sense, because words (recounters) and numbers (counters) are the pre-eminent symbols. This word is appropriate to the story of a miser; usury, interest, and the system of credit and debit constitute primary themes of the novel and display endless ironies. The frequent use of 'contar' repeatedly announces the code of story-telling itself, which both reflects and encompasses the other novelistic codes, including those that insinuate an ironic mode of reading.

In retrospect it becomes very evident that other individual words in this initial paragraph serve both to distribute and to collect multiple meanings in the story. Torquemada is first labeled 'inhumano' (which he is, of course, in the immediate sense of being a fiction). The constant plays on Torquemada's humanity or inhumanity are integrated with his vulgarized identification of God with 'Humanidad', and his self-serving conceptions of human kindness and charity. Yet although the narrator and the other characters continually call him 'inhumano', the story will reveal that he is tragically and comically human. Even within the satire, Torquemada's portrait employs numerous descriptive devices to present a personality which is as 'human' as that of Rosalía de Bringas.[3] His humanity becomes vulgarity (in two senses), but nonetheless counteracts his symbolic value. He is a man who could well move in the reader's own world, bridging the distance between fiction and reality, the symbolic and the everyday. The apparent meaning of the novel for the reader is closely associated with the covert negation of the description 'inhumano' and the consequent affirmation of his 'humanidad' (in both the individual and the global senses). *Torquemada en la hoguera* claims to be 'ejemplo' and 'enseñanza'. These terms conventionally bear an idealistic sense in literature and suggest a degree of abstraction from the real world. But this first, conventionally literary interpretation of 'ejemplo' and 'enseñanza', like 'contar' and 'inhumano', masks another. The meanings of these words do not remain separate from the reader's world in the realm of symbol and

metaphor. The manipulating *titiritero* manipulates not only the characters, but the reader too, so that the metaphorical distance separating
him from Torquemada discloses its illusiveness. The conventionally
moral and exemplary meanings are redirected in ways that permit the
reader, perhaps, to see his own irony reflected in that of the novel.

Torquemada en la hoguera offers no morally victorious or utterly
abhorrent character; no abstract 'moral' will emerge from it. Because
of the equivocation in applying conventional definitions of humanity
and inhumanity or tragedy and comedy to Torquemada, he is never
totally condemned. Nor is there any absolutely 'good' character; even
the poor but charitable *Tía Roma* is motivated by personal preference
in her kindness and does not hesitate to augment Torquemada's grief.
In *Torquemada en la hoguera* we find that there are no absolutes, either
in morality or in the process of reading. Even the notion of poetic justice
is thwarted because the reader finally comes to sympathize, at least
partially, with Torquemada – a figure irreducible to stereotyped social,
moral, or literary identities. The reversal of conventions involves a
reader who has either been educated in the novel's ironic *vraisemblance*,
or fallen victim to it. One ramification of the reader's inclusion in the
narrative strategy is the re-evaluation which he must make of commonplace meanings in literature and ultimately in life. Iser's comments on
Thackeray's *Vanity Fair* (a novel with a manipulating puppeteer) are
applicable to *Torquemada en la hoguera*; the reader, he observes, is
forced to make judgments about the novel which are just as real as
those he would make about his own world (Iser, especially pp. 112–13).
The ultimate production of meaning occurs in the reader's mind. It is
a process which can lead him to realize the superficial nature of his
previous ideas. This is a tacitly Cervantine operation; though we first
laugh at Quijote, we cannot escape recognizing finally that he is part
of us – or we of him.

The first sentence of the second paragraph of *Torquemada en la
hoguera* abruptly narrows the distance between character and reader:
'Mis amigos conocen ya, por lo que de él se me antojó referirles, a don
Francisco Torquemada, a quien algunos historiadores inéditos de estos
tiempos llaman *Torquemada el Peor*' (v. 906). The narrator's readers
are not only his accomplices ('mis amigos') but also those of 'el *Peor*'
of 'estos tiempos' whom they 'conocen ya'. The use of the present
tense, the first-person possessive, and other deictic terms such as 'ya'
and 'estos' continues throughout the paragraph (and the novel). These
recourses frequently include word plays such as 'si han tenido algo que

ver con él en cosa de más cuenta' (v. 906), where the derivatives of
'contar' again suggest more than one meaning. In his definition of
discours and *histoire*, Benveniste identifies the deictic features in verb
forms and in demonstratives which denote the 'here and now' and the
'I' of the discursive narration.[4] Because discourse contains the speaking
'yo', it also contains the listening 'tú' whom it addresses; the two exist
for each other.[5] Thus the novelistic discourse not only addresses the
'tú' of the reader, but makes him part of itself.

The first two paragraphs of *Torquemada en la hoguera* illustrate
how the novel constantly moves back and forth between *histoire* and
discours. The reader is no sooner placed at a secure distance from the
history, than he is abruptly drawn into the discourse and forced to
participate in it. This process occurs continually, even within individual
sentences. After enumerating the inhabitants of 'aquel infierno en que
fenecen desnudos y fritos los deudores' where Torquemada moves,
they are summed up as 'sujetos diversos que no aciertan a resolver el
problema aritmético en que se funda la existencia social, y otros muy
perdidos, muy faltones, muy destornadillados de cabeza o rasos de
moral, tramposos y embusteros' (v. 906). They are 'sujetos' in a double
sense, and so is the reader. The debtors with whom Torquemada deals
are characterized by various pejoratives that cover a range of socially
pretentious, but morally weak individuals, with whom the reader,
though perhaps not like them himself, cannot but be acquainted. The
reference to the 'problema aritmético en que se funda la existencia
social' implies a parody of the nineteenth-century 'dismal science' and
reinforces the integration of the monetary with the moral. The illusive
distance of the reader from the inhabitants of 'aquel infierno' further
evaporates in the first lines of the next paragraph: 'Pues todos éstos, el
bueno y el malo, el desgraciado y el pillo, cada uno por su arte propio,
pero siempre con su sangre y sus huesos, le amasaron al sucio de
Torquemada una fortunita que ya la quisieran muchos que se dan
lustre en Madrid' (v. 906). The deictic force of the demonstrative
'éstos' and the present tense 'se dan' approach the reader. The paradox
suggested in the qualification of 'arte propio' by 'sangre y huesos'
applies equally well to life and to narration. Together with 'le amasaron'
these phrases illustrate how the debtors themselves, and not Torquemada, created their own living hell. The approximation of the reader
to Torquemada's world reverses the apparently safe distance of the
novel's opening paragraph and reveals that the apostrophaic sentence
in the second paragraph is also ironic: ' ¡Ay de mis buenos lectores si

conocen al implacable fogonero de vidas y haciendas por tratos de otra clase, no tan sin malicia, no tan desinteresados como estas inocentes relaciones entre narrador y lector!' (v. 906). The 'inocentes relaciones' are not that at all; all statements, even individual words, are potentially misleading, especially the narrator's direct remarks to the reader. The reader may be deceived if he is not continually on guard for this ironic *vraisemblance*. These counterposed meanings appear at many levels of the text: in a word, in a symbolic allusion, in a sentence, in a portrait, in an historical account, and in all the literary and cultural codes which traverse the text. Finally, the traditional concept of moral exemplarity is manipulated. This novel has less to do with constructing a perfect moral *exemplum* than with identifying the conventions of reading which govern the texts of novel, society, and self.

In the last four paragraphs of chapter I we are given a brief history of Torquemada and his growing wealth. His life is parallel to the development of the middle class and its obsessively materialistic values – ontogeny recapitulates phylogeny, as it were. 'The evils of materialism' is one of the major themes in this novella and the entire *Torquemada* series; Torquemada is material progress personified, and its epitome. His portrait constitutes a detailed inventory of the materialistic preoccupations of nineteenth-century Spanish society. Thus, whatever the contemporary reader's final reaction to Torquemada might be, he reacts in part to his own world. The denomination 'el *Peor*' gives way to 'mi don Francisco' and other terms of varying familiarity or condemnation. The use of the imperfect or even present tenses replaces the perfective designation of events by the preterite. The narrator often assumes a personal acquaintance with the characters and events; he includes the reader by means of asides such as 'mis amigos' and the use of the first-person plural verb forms. The free indirect style, the narrator's appropriation of the character's thoughts or expressions, is employed throughout the novella; it often conveys a tone of humorous, parodical deprecation – especially through diminutives such as 'fortunita', 'veinticuatro habitacioncitas', 'regularcita', and colloquialisms such as 'bonitos préstamos', 'préstamos de lo fino, adelantos de lo gordo y vamos viviendo'. All these elements correspond more or less to the sort of *titiritero*, personalized narrator or 'pseudo-author', which Roy Pascal suggests was one of the two roles of the narrator in novels such as *Don Quijote*, *Tom Jones*, *Tristram Shandy*, or *Vanity Fair*. The other role was that of the non-personal, near-omniscient narrator who commonly employed the free indirect style in order to achieve greater intersubjective penetration into the characters of the novel. The pseudo-authorial and personalized narrator of *Torquemada en la hoguera* employs the free indirect style abusively when he mimics or recalls Torquemada's own words in order to parody and draw away from him in a more or less objective manner. This 'abusive' use of the free indirect style by the pseudo-author serves to produce, Pascal concludes, 'a great enrichment of the art of storytelling', at the same time as the pseudo-author's 'interventions jostle with the FIS forms, sometimes to disconcert the reader, cheat his expectations, and confuse him' (p. 77). Yet this very confusion is the essence of irony. It underlies the ambiguity of the free indirect style itself, as well as the interplay of the two roles of the narrator and the merger of illusion and reality. It makes the *exemplum* real, and renders the reader accountable for what the verb 'contar' recounts.

After the introduction and historical background given in chapter I, details of Torquemada's past are related, especially the death of his wife, Silvia. The narrator again steps in to speak directly to his reader: 'Perdónenme mis lectores si les doy la noticia sin la preparación conveniente, pues sé que apreciaban a doña Silvia, como la apreciábamos todos los que tuvimos el honor de tratarla y conocíamos sus excelentes prendas y circunstancias' (v. 907). The reader is drawn into the text as a participant in this discourse and as one who, he is told, already knew Doña Silvia. But the connotations of this sentence and of the succeeding passage are misleading. We are told of the couple's 'santa y laboriosa paz', and the double sense of 'santa' suggests both the religious and the cliché. But they are soon described as a 'pareja que podría servir de modelo a cuantas hormigas hay debajo de la tierra y encima de ella' (v. 907). This sentence appropriately ends the paragraph which began in praise of Silvia. Her 'excelentes prendas' were habits just as avaricious as Torquemada's: 'se habían compenetrado de un modo perfecto, llegando a ser ella otro él, y él como cifra y refundición de ambos' (v. 907). Thus, Silvia cannot have been any more 'appreciated' than her husband. The reader's comfortable complicity in the presentation of Silvia has been subverted. The 'honor' of knowing her is dubious indeed. Torquemada's grief over her death is also described humorously. He began to recover from his loss, and, 'aunque el recuerdo de su esposa no se extinguió en el alma del usurero, el dolor hubo de calmarse' (v. 907). If the reference to a usurer's soul is not barbed enough, the completion of the sentence insures its effect: 'los días fueron perdiendo lentamente su fúnebre tristeza; despejóse el sol

del alma, iluminando de nuevo las variadas combinaciones numéricas
que en ella había' (v. 907).

By now the identification of Torquemada's financial with his
spiritual condition is obvious. The preceding passage, like the mention
of him collecting rents on Sunday, poses the question of his personal
salvation. This is the dominant symbolic or religious concern of *Torquemada en la hoguera* (as well as of *Torquemada y San Pedro*) and
constitutes the nexus of its apparent exemplarity. The predominance of
the 'salvation motif' over the others is structurally corroborated in the
closing paragraph of chapter I. After describing the genius of Torquemada's twelve-year-old son Valentín, the narrator concludes:

Sólo he de afirmar ahora que el *Peor* no merecía tal joya, ¡qué había de
merecerla!, y que si fuese hombre capaz de alabar a Dios por los bienes
con que le agraciaba, motivos tenía el muy tuno para estarse, como
Moisés, tantísimas horas con los brazos levantados al cielo. No los levantaba, porque sabía que del cielo no había de caérle ninguna breva de las
que a él le gustaban. (v. 908)

Here is an explicit statement of Torquemada's inability to praise God.
It seems that he can only worship money – this is the *breva* he
appreciates. Moreover, the identification of Moses with Christ was a
commonplace of figural interpretation; yet the description of Valentín's
Christ-like nature and the suggestion, subsequently denied, of Torquemada's identity with Moses frustrate the reader's attempt to make such
interpretations. These sentences, and the last one of the novel, clearly
inscribe the religious symbolism which runs through the story. The
integration of this religious symbolism with the monetary motif suggests
that this code, like the others in the novel, is also inverted.

Throughout the novel the biblical text is recalled for parodic rather
than conventionally exemplary purposes, as in the reference to Moses.
Parody, Tomaschevsky observed, occurs against the background of
another literary tradition. *Torquemada en la hoguera*, though apparently structured as an *exemplum*, can actually be read as a counter-
genre. Unlike the parables of the New Testament. the recourses of
instruction employed in *Torquemada en la hoguera* are virtually
opposed to those of established tradition. The moral with which the
text begins is ironic. There is no 'morality' which emerges as absolute;
instead, the novella examines conventional immorality in order to
teach a new convention of reading. 'Some parodies', Tomaschevsky
writes, 'are developed freely for the sole purpose of showing off techniques.'[6] While this may not be Galdós' sole purpose – and questions of

intention must often remain moot – it does point to his highly sophisticated narrative techniques, and perhaps to the presence of irony for its own sake.

The figure of Valentín is a central focus of religious and explicitly biblical parody, especially since his death 'motivates' the story, just as Christ's does the New Testament. Valentín's representation as a Christ-figure is quite superficial. His introduction in the last paragraph of chapter 1 displays the major codes which traverse and center on his character, and foreshadows their importance for the novel. The initial description of his 'encantos', 'preciosidad tan extraordinaria', 'hechicera gravedad', and the 'rayo divino en sus ojos' (v. 908) is hyperbolic and suggests the symbolic, especially through terms such as 'divino'. Yet the hackneyed use of such words also subverts this tendency. Valentín's physical appearance is described next: 'Espigadillo de cuerpo, tenía las piernas delgadas, pero de buena forma; la cabeza, más grande de lo regular, con alguna deformidad en el cráneo' (v. 908). This movement from the symbolic to the material or from the idealized to the grotesque appears throughout the novel; it is the process by which the over-all story is made 'non-exemplary'. Montes Huidobro has noted of Galdós that 'su constante apego a la realidad, su deliberado deseo de ir de lo ideal a la realidad más turda, producen un desajuste típico que hace al símbolo una cosa palpable, cotidiana'.[7]

The other characters introduced in the first chapter do not escape parody either. We are told that Rufina, Torquemada's daughter, 'había sacado todas las capacidades domésticas de su madre, y gobernaba el hogar casi tan bien como ella' (v. 907). Rufina reproduces, almost completely, the miserly instincts of Silvia. The ensuing description appears favorable, if not patronizing, but we later see that Rufina also displays her father's traits. When Torquemada tells her that he has given his cape to a beggar, she immediately asks if it was his good one. The narrator proceeds to describe her bravery and selflessness at Valentín's bedside: 'Rendida de cansancio, Rufina no podía ya con su cuerpo... pero su valeroso espíritu la sostenía siempre en pie, diligente y amorosa como una hermana de caridad' (v. 922). Rufina's worry over which cape Torquemada gave away suggests, however, that her charity is not as totally indiscriminate and selfless as that of the Sisters of Charity. Even Rufina's boyfriend, who hardly figures in the 'story', is facetiously introduced in chapter 1: 'Era un *chico de Medicina*, chico en toda la extensión de la palabra, pues levantaba del suelo lo menos que puede levantar un hombre; estudiosillo, inocente, bonísimo y manchego por más señas' (v. 908). The diminutive 'estudiosillo' humorously and condescendingly reinforces the description of his short stature, and his *manchego* origin connotes a certain dull-wittedness.[8]

If, after the first chapter, the reader fails to become aware of the irony which pervades not only the characterizations, but the symbolism and the exemplary posture of the novel, then he is much more susceptible to manipulation in succeeding pages. Chapter II begins with the words 'Vamos a otra cosa', which recall the ever-present role of the narrator as puppeteer. The narrator describes exactly what type of usurer Torquemada is: 'don Francisco...no pudo eximirse de la influencia de esta segunda mitad del siglo XIX, que casi ha hecho una religión de las materialidades decorosas de la existencia...Viviendo el *Peor* en una época que arranca de la desamortización, sufrió, sin comprenderlo, la metamorfosis que ha desnaturalizado la usura metafísica, convirtiéndolo en positivista' (v. 908). Religion, contemporary history, and materialism are all conflated here. The conversion of metaphysics (or idealism) to positivism (or realism) is the process of this novel. The final words of the paragraph summarize the import of this information: 'que, en suma y para no cansar, la familia toda empezaba a tratarse como Dios manda' (v. 909). But the Torquemada family history can hardly be considered an example of Christian living, as the next passage reveals. The family's material progress is likened to a movement from conservative to liberal politics, and Torquemada expresses his satisfaction with his acquisitions as God expressed his satisfaction with the Creation: 'Y vió muy pronto don Francisco que aquellas novedades eran buenas' (v. 909). Torquemada, a symbol of materialist increase, is also a parodic representation of God, just as *Torquemada en la hoguera* parodies biblical and exemplary literature. Torquemada's blasphemous *muletillas*, 'biblias pasteleras' and 're-biblias', are humorous 're-inscriptions' of the novella's relation to Scripture. The reader who fails to recognize this intertextuality will also fail to comprehend their mutually parodic implications.

Torquemada's pride in his material *novedades* is parallel to that he feels for Valentín. His extreme pride in his young son's mathematical abilities is also linked, from chapter I on, with his un-Christian behavior. The first sentences depicting this father–son relationship suggest its vainglorious basis: 'En honor del tacaño, debe decirse que, si se conceptuaba reproducido físicamente en aquel pedazo de su propia naturaleza, sentía la superioridad del hijo, y por esto se congratulaba más de haberle dado el ser' (v. 910). Torquemada labels Valentín a 'divinidad' and applies such hackneyed hyperbolic epithets as 'gloria del mundo' to him. He believes, moreover, that he has more right than God has to Valentín, even though he claims that 'le hemos engendrado el padre eterno y yo'. This presumptive association of Torquemada with God ironically marks the gulf which actually separates them.

The physical and material likeness of Valentín to his father opposes the intellectual and spiritual likeness of Valentín to Christ. The latter likeness is explicit in the last paragraphs of chapter II, where the narrator's account of his education parallels the Gospel narrative of Jesus' youth. The chapter ends with Valentín among his professors, 'como Cristo niño entre los doctores' (v. 912), according to the narrator who also calls him 'angelito' and exclaims that 'su inocencia y celestial donosura casi nos permitían conocer a los ángeles como si los hubiéramos tratado' (v. 911). Yet one of Valentín's professors calls him the Antichrist, while another introduces him as 'el monstruo de la edad presente' (v. 911). The nature of Valentín's genius is fundamentally undecidable: 'Ese niño es cosa inexplicable, señor Torquemada: o tiene el diablo en el cuerpo o es el pedazo de divinidad más hermoso que ha caído en la tierra' (v. 910). For Torquemada there is no question that Valentín is 'un jirón excelso de la divinidad caído en la tierra' (v. 910). Yet the 'respeto supersticioso' which he feels for this 'ser sobrenatural' is the natural reaction, the narrator suggests, 'de lo que es materia frente a lo que es espíritu' (v. 910). Stated in these terms, the amazement of Torquemada, Valentín's teachers, and the narrator himself over the 'arte milagroso', 'inteligencia tan maravillosa', and 'magia' of this 'milagroso niño' is presented to the reader as a warning about the difficulty of distinguishing the material from the spiritual. This confusion of the material and the spiritual reflects the interpretation of literal and figural meanings in the novella. The reader who does not pause to consider the problematic significance of the label 'Newton resucitado' which Valentín's teachers apply to him will be unable to decipher the ironic intertextualities at each level of *Torquemada en la hoguera*.

Chapter III begins with another explicit reference to the hand of the novelistic *titiritero*:

Basta de matemáticas, digo yo ahora, pues me urge apuntar que Torquemada vivía en la misma case de la calle de Tudescos donde le conocimos cuando fué a verle la de Bringas para pedirle no recuerdo qué favor, allá por el 68, y tengo prisa por presentar a cierto sujeto que conozco hace tiempo y que hasta ahora nunca menté para nada: un don José Bailón, que iba todas las noches a la casa de nuestro don Francisco a jugar con él la partida de damas o de mus, y cuya intervención en mi cuento es necesaria ya para que se desarrolle con lógica. (v. 912)

This introduction describes the two contradictory but coexisting general phenomena which embrace the tension of the novel as a whole: it invokes conventional and literary exemplarity while at the same time negating them. The passage first suggests an autonomous reality; Bailón exists and the story is plausible. We 'real' beings, as accomplices of the narrator, lend our reality to Bailón and his story. On the other hand, the sheer conventionality of the process just described, like the Cervantine 'no quiero acordarme', implies an intensely literary reinscription. This constant movement between the two realms seems to achieve a merger of fiction and reality. The portrait of Bailón is an index of the text's awareness of its own literary and rhetorical nature as well as a major element in its code of religious and philosophical references. Like the word 'contar', the character Bailón joins two seemingly disparate codes.

Bailón foments the pseudo-religious beliefs which come to motivate Torquemada's actions. Nearly an entire chapter is devoted to the portrait of Bailón, which overtly parodies clerical ignorance and depravity, as well as popular religious sentimentality and simplistic philosophical notions then in vogue. Bailón, a renegade priest, thus already figuring among the excommunicate, joined the Protestants, lived with a woman, and finally becomes a usurer. Hence he is rightly referred to as 'el condenado' and 'dado a los demonios', colloquialisms whose eschatological implications ominously overwhelm their more ordinary sense. His teachings about a sort of pantheistic God, 'Humanidad', are an implicit parody of *krausismo*, which is thus drawn into the network of intertextual relations that *Torquemada en la hoguera* elaborates between itself, pop philosophy, the Bible, and Catholic dogma. Bailón also believes in reincarnation, another notion adopted by Torquemada and further developed in the later *Torquemada* novels.

The description of Bailón's ideas is prefaced with these comments: 'Don José era de los que con cuatro ideas y pocas más palabras se las componen para aparentar que saben lo que ignoran y deslumbrar a los ignorantes sin malicia. El más deslumbrado era don Francisco, y además el único mortal que leía los folletos babilónicos a los diez años de publicarse' (v. 913). Bailón's writings, like his spoken advice, are fundamentally depraved – 'babilónicos'. Yet despite their blasphemous

content, their style maintains a certain relationship to that of Scripture:
'Escribía Bailón aquellas necedades en parrafitos cortos, y a veces
rompía con una cosa muy santa: verbigracia: "Gloria a Dios en las
alturas y paz, etcétera..."' (v. 913). The transition which the word
'verbigracia' effects between the narrator's 'cosa muy santa' and
Bailón's stupidities marks the relation of Scripture to *Torquemada en
la hoguera* itself. The same intertextual principle founds Bailón's
'bobadas escritas en estilo bíblico' and the novella's biblical allusions.
The character of Bailón is a locus for the interplay of sacred and pro-
fane codes of meaning. For a while he had lived 'muy a lo bíblico,
amancebado con una viuda rica que tenía rebaño de cabras...
Cuento todo esto como me lo contaron, reconociendo que en esta parte
de la historia patriarcal de Bailón hay gran oscuridad' (v. 912). His
having lived 'muy a lo bíblico' is even more ironic since he was a
priest. The plays on 'contar' here and the invocation of the historical
chronicle reinforce the literariness of this character, a pamphlet-writer.
The description of his physical appearance also enhances this literariness, while subverting the symbolic value which it would possess as a
traditionally literary *exemplum*. Bailón's features suggest something
between 'un Dante echado a perder' and 'la síbila de Cumas' (v. 913).
The scarcely coherent pronouncements of Torquemada's sybil are
damningly unorthodox. The consequences of Bailón's teachings for
Torquemada are especially important because of his subsequent reaction to his son's illness. Although Torquemada is the 'único mortal
que leía los folletos babilónicos', he understands little of what Bailón
says:

Lo único que don Francisco sacaba de toda aquella monserga era que
Dios es la Humanidad, y que la Humanidad es la que nos hace pagar
nuestras picardías o nos premia por nuestras buenas obras. Lo demás no lo
entendía así le ahorcaran. El sentimiento católico de Torquemada no
había sido nunca muy vivo...Pues después de viudo las pocas ideas del
Catecismo que el *Peor* conservaba en su mente, como papeles o apuntes
inútiles, las barajó con todo aquel fárrago de la Humanidad–Dios,
haciendo un lío de mil demonios. (v. 914)

The association between Torquemada's materialistic concept of re-
demption and the colloquial expression 'un lío de mil demonios' marks
a connection between Bailón's spiritual teachings and Valentín's
physical health. Valentín's illness is introduced with a reference to the
'diabolical' hold of Bailón's doctrines over Torquemada's mind, which
was 'siempre atento a la baja realidad de sus negocios. Pero llegó un

día...en que tales ideas hubieron de posesionarse de su mente con cierta tenacidad' (v. 914).

The above passage, which signals the beginning of the novelistic 'action', precipitates the association in Torquemada's mind, and in the narrative structure, between religious values (or more precisely charity – a topic of increasing preoccupation in Galdós from Guillermina to Benina) and Valentín's illness (or God's justice). Torquemada's initial reaction to this turn of events foreshadows corollary motifs. He becomes almost dumbstruck, a reaction greatly intensified later, thus increasing the diabolical connotations which surround him. However, his grief is not focussed on his son *per se*, but rather on his extraordinary abilities – especially his mathematical genius. Torquemada is moved to tears by his son's computations. He enters Valentín's room, 'donde se le presentaba ante los ojos, oprimiéndole el corazón, el encerado en que Valentín trazaba con tiza sus problemas matemáticos...que casi le hicieron llorar como una música triste' (v. 915). This passage implicitly associates Torquemada's usury with his love for his son; both involve calculations of his interests. The poetic impulse behind the simile 'como una música triste' contrasts with the prosaic object of his emotion. When Torquemada contemplates the beauty of the heavens and its multitude of stars, he appreciates their beauty by imagining how Valentín could calculate their value for him as if they were coins:

Corriendo hacia su casa, en retirada, miraba al cielo, cosa en él muy contraria a la costumbre, pues si alguna vez lo miró para enterarse del tiempo, jamás, hasta aquella noche, lo había contemplado. ¡Cuantísima estrella! ...hermosas y graves, millones de millones de miradas que no aciertan a ver nuestra pequeñez. Lo que más suspendía el ánimo del tacaño era la idea de que todo aquel cielo estuviese indiferente a su gran dolor, o más bien ignorante de él...Las había chicas, medianas y grandes; algo así como pesetas, medios duros y duros. Al insigne prestamista le pasó por la cabeza lo siguiente: 'Como se ponga bueno me ha de ajustar esta cuenta: si acuñáramos todas las estrellas del cielo, ¿cuánto producirían al cinco por ciento de interés compuesto en los siglos que van desde que todo eso existe?' (v. 921)

The mordant irony which these calculations of the stars' interest call forth is reinforced by such incongruous phrases as 'el ánimo del tacaño' and 'insigne prestamista'. At this point, the reader must decide how he will construe a sympathetic presentation of Torquemada. Torquemada's grief has made him more contemplative and aware of his humanity; it is the first time that he has raised his sights from his 'baja realidad' to consider an existence higher than his own. He feels the utter insignificance and pain of being ignored by the heavens, a sentiment which, however vain, is nonetheless pathetically human. These sentences, related partially in the free indirect style, may evoke a sense of both irony and sympathy from the reader. The coexistence of these two attitudes contributes to the over-all tension of the text and its reading. The confusion of irony and sympathy in this account of Torquemada's meditations illustrates well Pascal's suggestion (p. 42) that 'sometimes the character's self-delusion is so deeply rooted in essential character and the inevitable ambiguity of life that the irony is wholly sympathetic and approaches tragic pathos'.

Valentín is especially precious to Torquemada because he will be the greatest mind of his age, a great engineer, another Newton; consequently, 'Torquemada sería en tal caso la segunda persona de la Humanidad; y sólo por la gloria de haber engendrado al gran matemático sería cosa de plantarle en un trono' (v. 919). Finally, after Valentín's death, Torquemada expresses his feeling of loss by kissing the blackboard where some of his son's calculations remain:

el inconsolable padre fué al comedor y descolgó el encerado en que estaban aún escritos los problemas matemáticos, y tomándolo por retrato que fielmente le reproducía las facciones del adorado hijo, estuvo larguísimo rato dando besos sobre la fría tela negra, y estrujándose la cara contra ella, con lo que la tiza se le pegó al bigote mojado de lágrimas, y el infeliz usurero parecía haber envejecido súbitamente. Todos los presentes se maravillaron de esto, y hasta se echaron a llorar. (v. 935)

Torquemada has this blackboard framed in gold, and in the later novels this icon becomes part of a shrine which he erects in Valentín's memory and to which he prays – a further indication of his distorted and unorthodox religious values. This bathetic scene again contains its element of compassion; Torquemada's grief is real, despite its focus on numbers and calculations. The identification of Valentín with his calculations defines explicitly the assimilation of numerical (materialistic, mundane) motifs to the conventional code of religious values. Because Valentín is the second Christ and the second Newton, the faith which he inspires in his father, his legacy to the modern age, combines Christian charity with mathematical calculation. The conjunction of religious and economic themes in the figure of Valentín is reaffirmed in the last line of chapter III after he falls ill. Valentín passes a troubled night with 'el habla insegura, las ideas desenhebradas, como cuentas de un rosario cuyo hilo se rompe' (v. 915). The state of Valentín's mental processes reflects Torquemada's religious values, which, like the beads ('cuentas') of a broken rosary, no longer allow a proper reckoning ('cuenta'). In these passages numbers, mathematical symbols, usurp the functions and value of religious symbols. They do this in the same way as words, verbal symbols, replace what is taken for reality. Within *Torquemada en la hoguera*, both numbers and words, thematically expressed in usury and charity, materialism and religion, eventually become indistinguishable. Having appropriated the functions of religious symbolism and reality, as well as their associated cultural and social codes, the numbers and words of the text merge their own functions in that of a single term, 'contar'. The reader's attempts to distinguish among these various functions, in what has become a homogeneous symbolic system, invariably require an arbitrary, and hence essentially ironic, separation of the story from its telling or of language from reality.

Chapter IV describes Torquemada's first efforts to save Valentín's life: 'El desasosiego, la inquietud nerviosa, el desvarío del tacaño sin ventura, no se pueden describir' (v. 915). This sentence seeks to describe human grief by attributing to it an existence beyond the realm of fiction, beyond language, thereby making it seem more 'real'. Here, in a series of fluctuating meditations, Torquemada rejects recognizing his sins, which he admits might have led to Valentín's illness. Like his love for his son, Torquemada's attempts to save him are based on calculation. He continually declares that he will save Valentín, 'cueste lo que cueste', and even after his death vows to 'resucitarle costara lo que costase' (v. 935). Torquemada bargains with God through charitable acts calculated to purchase his son's life. His attitude is outlined in this monologue which occurs during the initial stages of Valentín's illness:

He faltado a la Humanidad, y esa muy tal y cual me las cobra ahora con los réditos atrasados...No; pues si Dios, o quienquiera que sea, me lleva mi hijo, ¡me voy a volver más malo, más perro...!...Pero no, ¡qué disparates digo!...Si me pones bueno a mi hijo, yo no sé que cosas haría; pero ¡qué cosas tan magníficas y tan...! Pero ¿quién es el sinvergüenza que dice que no tengo apuntada ninguna buena obra? (v. 916)

The tenor of these reflections (like the rest of the paragraph and the other meditations), is one of self-accusation combined with a determination to do better; yet it includes an ominous threat. Torquemada's good intentions are undermined by the fact that he threatens God. His subsequent efforts are invalidated because he cannot disassociate his endeavors from the structure of usury. The worst of his faults is that he always demands a *pagaré*, even from God. Nevertheless, his misguided conduct may arouse sympathy in the reader as well as humor, especially because he is unaware of his miserly attitude. He never totally accepts his guilt, because he cannot recognize any injustice in his usurous enterprises.

Torquemada's first acts of charity circumscribe the pattern of all the others. During his Sunday rent collection he becomes progressively less demanding with each tenant, even to the point of being somewhat charitable; he temporarily returns part of one poor woman's rent so that she can buy food. He maintains all the time that he does not want praise for his acts, but his words are extremely revealing; for example:

Deja, déjate el dinero...O mejor, para que no lo tomes a desaire, partámoslo y quédate con venticinco reales...Ya me los darás otro día... ¡Bribonazas, cuando debíais confesar que soy para vosotras como un padre, me tacháis de inhumano y de qué sé yo qué! No, yo les aseguro a todas que respeto a la Humanidad, que la considero, que la estimo, que ahora y siempre haré todo el bien que pueda y un poquito más...
...No necesito que nadie me dé bombo...Piojosas, para nada quiero vuestras gratitudes...Me paso por las narices vuestras bendiciones. (v. 917–18)

He does indeed desire praise; his continual denials only serve to confirm this. Throughout this chapter there are plays on his conception of 'Humanidad', 'humano', and 'inhumano'. The recipients of this half-hearted charity are astounded. They cannot believe the change that has come over the man and associate his behavior with the appearance of a comet: 'Ahí tenéis por qué está saliendo todas las noches en el cielo esa estrella con rabo. Es que el mundo se va a acabar' (v. 918). Apocalyptic symbolism and vulgar superstition are joined by a single image. The final lines of chapter IV firmly identify the opposing forces determining Torquemada's actions: 'Todas le miraban por la escalera abajo, y por el patio adelante, y por el portal afuera, haciendo unos gestos tales que parecía el mismo demonio persignándose' (v. 918). This incongruous picture of the devil crossing himself once again confuses the holy and the diabolical codes for the reader's interpretation.

After thus attempting to reform his rent collection, Torquemada runs home in chapter V to see if Valentín's condition has improved: 'El corazón dió en decirle que encontraría buenas noticias (v. 918). But Valentín is not better, a fact which belies the true inspiration of Torquemada's 'corazón', another key term in the narration. Torquemada cannot face his son's illness, the narrator tells us, 'sin duda por causa de su deficiencia moral; se sentía medroso, consternado, y como responsable de tanta desventura y dolor tan grande' (v. 918–19). In other novels we have seen that the use of 'sin duda' by the narrator often has ironic effects; it serves to negate what it supposedly affirms at the same time as it assumes the reader's agreement.[9] In this case the narrator's judgment of Torquemada is misleadingly simplistic; the reader may not consider his reaction so uncommon in times of grief and desperation.

The free indirect style is used in its most common forms, interrogation and exclamation, to communicate Torquemada's confusion about why Providence should punish Valentín's innocent genius:

¡Llevarse al niño, lumbrera de la ciencia, y dejar acá todos los tontos! ¿Tenía esto sentido común? ¿No había motivo para rebelarse contra los de arriba, ponerlos como ropa de pascua y mandarlos a paseo?...Si Valentín se moría, ¿qué quedaba en el mundo? Oscuridad, ignorancia. Y para el padre, ¡qué golpe! ¡Porque figurémonos todo lo que sería don Francisco cuando su hijo, ya hombre, empezase a figurar, a confundir a todos los sabios..! Nada, nada, envidia pura, envidia...Pero..., pero...¿y si no fuese envidia, sino castigo? (v. 919)

Torquemada appreciates only profit and common sense; thus he sees the actions of 'Humanidad' as wholly unreasonable and perhaps based on 'envidia' of his gains as the father of Valentín. Yet Torquemada also recognizes that it may be a 'castigo' for his own sins, which, although he doubts that he has any, he proposes to correct; Torquemada, like all the ironic characters in Galdós' novels, cannot see himself. There are numerous word plays in this passage, such as 'figurémonos cuando...empezase a figurar', which applies the various senses of 'figurar' to Valentín. The verb 'figurar', like 'contar', also possesses a discursive and an arithmetical meaning, which are employed simultaneously here. Torquemada's presumptuously banal proposal to dismiss the gods, which he incongruously expresses with a colloquial reference to religious ceremony ('ropa de pascua'), has potentially diabolical consequences: were his rebellion to fail – or perhaps if it were to suceed – Torquemada would become a new Lucifer, and the materialist society around him a new hell.

Torquemada approaches the bed where Valentín lies delirious:

Puso atención a las expresiones incoherentes del delirio, y le oyó decir: 'Equis elevado al cuadrado menos uno partido por dos, más cinco... Papá, papá la característica del logaritmo de un entero tiene tantas unidades menos una, como...' Ningún tormento de la Inquisición iguala al

que sufría Torquemada oyendo estas cosas. Eran las pavesas del asom-
broso entendimiento de su hijo revolando sobre las llamas en que éste se
consumía. (v. 920)

The greatest torment for Torquemada is to hear his son calculate
deliriously. These sentences repeat the motif of the Inquisition with
which the story began, employing the same metaphors. But here
Valentín is a victim of the flames, along with Torquemada. Torquemada subsequently leaves to distribute alms: 'Salió como si fuera en
persecución de un deudor...con paso de inglés tras de su víctima'
(v. 920). He pursues the performance of charity like the collection of
debts. The chapter ends as a poor, half-naked beggar, whom Torquemada likens to San Pedro, approaches him: 'Torquemada pasó de
largo, y se detuvo a poca distancia; volvió hacia atrás, estuvo un rato
vacilando, y al fin siguió su camino. En el cerebro le fulguró esta idea:
"Si conforme traigo la capa nueva, trajera la vieja"' (v. 921). Torquemada's charity is never completely selfless. Chapter vi opens with the
words: 'Y al entrar en su casa: —¡Maldito de mí! No debí dejar
escapar aquel acto de cristiandad' (v. 921). These words bear an ironic
as well as a literal sense; Torquemada is damned for missing charitable
opportunities and for his selfish pursuit of them. He recriminates himself as though he had allowed a debtor to escape, and then returns to
the street in search of 'San Pedro', this time wearing his old cape.
Afterwards, when *Tía Roma*, the ugly old rag-collector of the house,
tells Torquemada to pray and to be good, he responds:

> —¿Qué sabes tú, *Tía Roma*? —dijo Torquemada poniéndose lívido—
> ...¿Acaso piensas tú que yo soy tirano y perverso, como creen los tontos y
> algunos perdidos, malos pagadores?...Pero Dios sabe la verdad...Si he
> hecho o no he hecho caridades en estos días, eso no es cuenta de nadie: no
> me gusta que me averigüen y pongan en carteles mis buenas acciones.
> (v. 922)

All of Torquemada's words bear double meanings. What he says, that
God knows the truth and that his charity should not be publicized, is
of course entirely valid – but the reader may readily perceive another
reason for applying this dictum to Torquemada's variety of charitable
activity.

When Bailón comes to comfort Torquemada, his philosophies are
essentially reduced to a vague injunction to observe the Golden Rule.
Torquemada rejects this as irrelevant, saying 'si se me muere, lo mismo
me da lo blanco que lo negro' (v. 923). Torquemada neglects, ignores,
and rejects distinctions of moral values which are as clear as black and

white, perhaps a comment on Bailón's influence. Then, 'En aquel momento oyóse un grito áspero, estridente, lanzado por Valentín, y que a entrambos los dejó suspensos de terror. Era el grito meníngeo, semejante al alarido del pavo real' (v. 923). Torquemada's venally utilitarian attitude is answered by the scream which signals Valentín's imminent expiration. (The peacock, notably, symbolized Christ in early Christian art.) The narrator then observes: 'el coloquio con la *Tía Roma* y con don José, el grito de Valentín, y he aquí que al judío le da como una corozonada, se le enciende en la mollera fuego de inspiración' (v. 924). Torquemada is inspired to 'help' one of his perpetual debtors, Don Juan. We are given a brief history of Don Juan; because of his wife's outrageous expenses in order to appear well in society, and Don Juan's own frivolous nature, he is deservedly (the narrator intimates) far into debt. Torquemada, in the name of 'charity', now offers Don Juan an interest-free loan, guaranteed by the collateral of his valuable furniture, of course. Don Juan rejects this proposal because he has just secured another loan. His disdain for Torquemada's offer amazes and offends the miser, who responds: 'Don Juan, don Juan, sepa usted, si no lo sabe, que yo también tengo mi humanidad como cualquier hijo de vecino, que me intereso por el prójimo y hasta que favorezco a los que me aborrecen. Usted me odia, don Juan, usted me detesta, no me lo niegue, porque no me puede usted pagar; esto es claro' (v. 926). Torquemada's insensitivity to the non-materialistic import of the Christian precepts which he invokes – 'me interesa por el prójimo' and 'favorezco a los que me aborrecen' – contrasts with his acute awareness of the materialist motives of his society. The play on the word 'interés' accelerates at this point.

Torquemada's charitable actions are all presented in a more or less overtly ironic light. Perhaps the most detailed of these, and the one most neglected so far by critics of *Torquemada en la hoguera*, is the episode involving Torquemada, Isidora Rufete, and her consumptive lover, an artist named Martín. The resuscitation of this heroine of *La desheredada* alerts the reader to what may perhaps be another level of irony. The literariness of Isidora's quixotic character is perpetuated in this novella, and supports the fusion of sympathetic humanity and exemplary caricature in the portrait of Torquemada. The colloquial reference to her 'novelesco pasado' is a call for the reader to make these literary associations, as is her subsequent appeal, 'pongámonos en la realidad' (v. 927). Isidora's exhortation parodies Torquemada's own manner of expression, an element of his characterization in the novel, at the same time as it self-reflectively identifies its fiction as fiction.

The usurer visits the tiny attic room of the couple after leaving Don Juan; they receive him as a divine deliverer. Torquemada calls the money which he lends to them a gift, does not even require a promissory note, and dramatically tears up before their eyes the one which they offer. Yet his habitual demand for some form of collateral leads him to take a few of Martín's paintings, for the 'safe keeping' of these works which he professes to appreciate so greatly, as he calculates their posthumous value. The presentation of Torquemada in this scene is extremely satirical. His cynical asides indicate exactly the depth of his 'generous' sentiments. As he enters their miserable dwelling he expresses his compassion for them: ' ¡Lástima de muchacho! Tan buen pintor y tan mala cabeza... ¡Habría podido ganar tanto dinero!' (v. 926). It is not that Torquemada does not feel pity, but simply that his reaction always concerns the 'material' aspects of things. When the couple explain that they need money to enable Martín to recuperate in the country, Torquemada says to himself: 'Al campo santo es donde tú vas prontito' (v. 927). When Martín indicates that they are expecting 500 *pesos* from his aunt, Torquemada thinks 'Como no te mande tu tía quinientos puñales' (v. 928). Finally, as in other cases, Torquemada's charity is not even superficially wholehearted; they request 3,000 *reales* and he gives them 2,800: 'Tiene ahí ciento cuarenta duros, o sean dos mil ochocientos reales...' (v. 929). Throughout this scene there is also an interesting series of word plays on the terms 'interés', 'corazón', 'humano', and 'cuenta'. Torquemada considers himself one of 'los hombres de corazón blando' (v. 927) and refers to 'ese corazón tierno que me ha dado Dios' (v. 928). When Isidora and Martín ask for the money, Torquemada responds: 'Piénselo bien y ajuste sus cuentas. Yo estoy decidido a protegerlos... hasta el sacrificio y hasta quitarme el pan de la boca para que ustedes maten el hambre, pero... reparen que debo mirar... por mis intereses...' (v. 928). Isidora and Martín offer to pay any interest which Torquemada might demand, but he replies: '—No me refiero al materialismo del rédito del dinero, sino a mis intereses, claro, a mis intereses.'

The irony of the portraits of Isidora and Martín in this scene is as intense as that of Torquemada. Their appreciation of the *tacaño* reveals the true nature of their own characters; they love money almost as much as he does. Isidora's life revolves around the power money holds over a person, just as in her own novel. Her previous habits are humorously recalled by the fact that, despite her abject

poverty, she still buys bonded paper, pen and ink. When the narrator
pretends to be most sympathetic toward her, he parodically calls forth
La desheredada. For example, the exclamation ' ¡Dios, qué botas, y
cómo desfiguraban aquel pie tan bonito!' (v. 924) alludes to another
episode with its own complex of moral and stylistic allusions: when
Isidora admires her new boots and small feet, the narrator insinuates
her vanity and impracticality by the use of a Cervantine chronicle
device.[10] When Torquemada places the money in their hands at the
end of chapter VII, Isidora and Martín are overwhelmed; chapter VIII
begins: 'Al ver el dinero, Isidora casi lloraba de gusto, y el enfermo se
animó tanto, que parecía haber recobrado la salud' (v. 929). This
intense, emotional involvement with money entirely determines their
moral and social behavior, as the narrator immediately indicates
through a short history of their relationship:

¡Pobrecillos, estaban tan mal, habían pasado tan horribles escaseces y
miserias! Dos años antes se conocieron en casa de un prestamista que a
entrambos los desollaba vivos. Se confiaron su situación respectiva, se
compadecieron y se amaron: aquella misma noche durmió Isidora en el
estudio...El amor les hizo llevadera la desgracia. Se casaron en el ara del
amancebamiento, y a los dos días de unión se querían de veras. (v. 929)

The use of the diminutive 'pobrecillos' belies the ironic significance of
the narrator's pretended sympathy in these lines. Isidora and Martín
have been brought together by money, or rather the lack of it, and
they pity each other. The monetary origin of this mutual pity establishes a parallel between their situation and Torquemada's. Torquemada continually asks them to have compassion on him because of his
sick son. He also claims that he deserves their prayers and blessings
because he gives them money. Isidora's and Martín's admiration for
Torquemada is a commentary on their own characters and the values
which motivate them; what really attracts them is his money. The
reader will put himself at a distance from this scene when he recognizes the absurdity of their praises for Torquemada's generosity, and
the distortions of their values.

Like Torquemada, Isidora and Martín are usually mistaken in their
judgments. Martín tells Torquemada: 'Don Francisco...es usted la
persona más cristiana, más completa y más humanitaria que hay bajo
el sol' (v. 928). Martín repeatedly vows that Valentín will recover
because his 'corazón' tells him so, just as Torquemada is so often mis-
advised by his heart. Isidora says: 'Me parece que Dios le ha de
favorecer, le ha de premiar sus buenas obras' (v. 929). She too con-

siders good works a means to a reward, which her other remarks reveal
to be just as worldly and materialistically conceived as Torquemada's.
His advice to them suggests the ultimate irony of this scene: '—Hijos
míos, sed buenos y que os aproveche el ejemplo que os doy. Favoreced
al pobre, amad al prójimo, y así como yo os he campadecido, com-
padecedme a mí, porque soy muy desgraciado' (v. 929). This synthesis
of Christ's words crowns the parody of the figure of Torquemada, who
associates Christian virtue with the most calculated acts of charity.
The reader who fails to appreciate the incongruity of these words in
Torquemada's mouth might likewise fail to understand the hypocrisy
of his own society's standards. Moreover, Torquemada is 'desgraciado'
in the literal and figurative sense of the word; he surely does not enjoy
God's grace either spiritually or materially. His unthinking use of this
term reflects the definitions of morality in his society.

   The fact that not only Torquemada but all the characters who
populate *Torquemada en la hoguera* demonstrate such ironic traits
intimates the permeation of material preoccupations throughout the
various levels of society in the novel. This concern with materialism
pervades Galdós' works, but is especially developed as a common
element of all social classes in the *Torquemada* series. In the later
novels Torquemada's sister-in-law, Cruz del Águila, displays an aristocratic avarice which is almost greater than his own. Torquemada's
wife, Fidela, seems virtuous, yet is principally concerned with her
personal comfort and objects to none of Torquemada's money-making
enterprises. San Pedro, the chaplain so-named by Torquemada because of his resemblance to the beggar of *Torquemada en la hoguera*,
is a paragon of saintliness, yet he is immersed in the materialistic life of
the aristocracy.[11] No one escapes this dual presentation in the series,
not even *Tía Roma*.

   Tía Roma comes to the fore in chapter VIII after Torquemada tells
her that he will offer a pearl to the Virgen del Carmen if she heals
Valentín.[12] Torquemada becomes even more generous after the episode
with Isidora and Martín, for when he returns home he learns that
Valentín's condition has improved. Besides the bribe to the Virgen,
Torquemada's elation leads him to offer *Tía Roma* a long-belated
token of appreciation – his old mattress. The scene which follows
incorporates many plays on 'contar' in describing *Tía Roma*'s reaction
to these bribes and 'gifts' and clearly delineates the extent of Torquemada's past miserliness. But it also reveals her own unforgiving bitter-
ness and lack of compassion for Torquemada in his grief, since she does

not hesitate to intensify his anguish by recalling his previous abuses. Unlike Benina, *Tía Roma* does not forgive those who wrong her; her resentment is deep-seated. She refuses Torquemada's mattress because she superstitiously fears that his diabolical nature will pass through it into her. Torquemada is infuriated by this rejection and by her accusation that he is attempting to cheat heaven. He curses her and the chapter closes thus: 'El demonio está contigo, y maldita tú eres entre todas las brujas y esperpentos que hay en el cielo...digo, en el infierno' (v. 933). This pronouncement of Torquemada (which parodies the Ave Maria), like all his judgments which do not concern purely monetary matters, is also misguided. *Tía Roma*, though not herself faultless, represents here a kind of messenger angel, while Torquemada is the possessed spirit. Thus *Tía Roma* is resentful, ignorant, and ugly, yet possesses certain prophetic abilities; on the other hand, Bailón is physically attractive and displays great pseudo-erudition, but his prophecies prove false.

Immediately after Torquemada verbally abuses *Tía Roma*, another prophetic event occurs. Chapter IX opens with Torquemada in an insane fury: 'Iba de una parte a otra...cual si le persiguieran sombras; daba cabezadas contra la pared, algunas tan fuertes que resonaban en toda la casa' (v. 933). These frenzies are greatly intensified upon Valentín's death. They are not only measures of his grief, but indicate the demoniacal associations which surround him. Valentín worsens and the 'grito de pavo real' is heard again; the cause and effect relation between Torquemada's horrible behavior and his son's condition is made clear. When Bailón tries to calm him by appealing for resignation, Torquemada again becomes furious; he is not rebelling, he claims, but is within his rights as a father: '—Yo no me rebelo, ¡puñales!, yo no me rebelo. Es que no quiero, no quiero dar a mi hijo, porque es mío, sangre de mi sangre y hueso de mis huesos...' (v. 933). Bailón tries to soothe him with his pseudo-religious philosophies: '—Valor, amigo mío, valor. En estos casos se conocen las almas fuertes. Acuérdese usted de aquel gran Filósofo que expiró en una cruz dejando consagrados los principios de la Humanidad' (v. 934). Torquemada, enraged and foaming at the mouth, attacks Bailón with 'un vigor muscular inverosímil'. At that point Valentín dies and Torquemada faints.

Torquemada's grief upon his son's death is real: 'cayó en profundísimo abatimiento físico y moral. Lloraba en silencio y daba unos suspiros que se oían en toda la casa' (v. 934). The moralizing overtones

of the narration are apparent, yet it remains within the realm of the
familiar and the plausible, unlike the traditional type of exemplary
novel. In planning Valentín's funeral, Torquemada recalls his charitable actions, and considers how little they achieved:

Vean de qué le vale a uno ser más bueno que el pan, y sacrificarse por los
desgraciados, y hacer bien a los que no nos pueden ver ni en pintura...
Total, que lo que pensaba emplear en favorecer a cuatro pillos... ¡mal
empleado dinero...! digo que esos dinerales los voy a gastar en hacerle a
mi hijo de mi alma, a esa gloria, a ese pródigo que no parecía de este
mundo, el entierro más lucido que en Madrid se ha visto. (v. 935)

The colloquialism 'ni en pintura' literally suggests Martín the painter,
while 'no nos pueden ver' suggests Torquemada's tenants and Don
Juan. All the colloquialisms used in *Torquemada en la hoguera* are
ironically applied in order to invest what is meaningless (from over-use)
with meaning, which the reader, accustomed to these set phrases, may
ignore. Torquemada's proposal to provide Valentín with a lavish
funeral casts doubt on the sincerity of a common practice, which contemporary society had come to regard as 'único bálsamo de pena'.
Moreover, it confirms the vanity of Torquemada and of all materialism,
in the face of death. This parody of funerary extravagances is intensified in *Torquemada y San Pedro* when Cruz hires 'nearly all of
Madrid' to participate in Fidela's funeral. Torquemada's grief is
depicted so vividly here that it cannot but evoke some compassion from
the reader, even if he is repulsed by the grotesque figure. Additionally,
he must necessarily recognize some similarity between the practices of
his own society and Torquemada's plans for an extravagant funeral.
The 'poetic justice' of this story is not fulfilled in the conventional
sense because the reader cannot totally separate himself from Torquemada or his world, and therefore cannot totally condemn Torquemada
without condemning himself, or at least his own world.

   After Torquemada recovers from his initial grief over Valentín's
death, 'la fiebre de los negocios terrenos' returns (having been temporarily replaced by a spiritual 'negocio'). *Tía Roma* 'entró a llevarle el
chocolate al gran inquisidor' only to find him furiously at work
'escribiendo números con mano febril'. She reproves him, saying
'—Nunca aprende...Ya está otra vez preparando los trastos de
ahorcar. Mala muerte va usted a tener, condenado de Dios, si no se
enmienda' (v. 936). He responds with a yellow glare, 'por ser en él de
este color lo que en los demás humanos ojos es blanco'. He replies:
'—Yo hago lo que me da mi santísima gana, so mamarracho, vieja

más vieja que la Biblia. Lucido estaría si consultara con tu necedad lo que debo hacer' (v. 936). The self-parody of Torquemada's words is again evident, especially in the terms 'santísima', 'Biblia', and 'lucido'; there is little humor now, however. Contemplating his figures, Torquemada appropriately ends his own novella:

—Si preparo los trastos, eso no es cuenta tuya ni de nadie, que yo me sé cuanto hay que saber de tejas abajo y aun de tejas arriba, ¡puñales! Ya sé que me vas a salir con el materialismo de la misericordia...A eso te respondo que si buenos memoriales eché, buenas y gordas calabazas me dieron. La misericordia que yo tenga, ¡puñales!, que me la claven en la frente. (v. 936)

This last paragraph summarily invokes the major codes which traverse the text – of religion and morality, of money and materialism, and of the conventions of narration itself. These are designated in the words 'misericordia', 'materialismo', and 'cuenta'. 'Eso no es cuenta tuya' once again, and finally, provides us with the dual sense of the word 'cuenta' that pervades the narrative: that of a tally sheet as well as a story. 'Memoriales' reinforces this duality: letters pleading favor or grace, or notebooks. Torquemada maintained a mental reckoning of his charitable credits and debits with God alongside his ledgers for usury and rent collection. To him, there never was any focus to charity except the 'materialismo de la misericordia'. The reader might, in spite of himself, see parallels between his own world and that of the 'ferocious victim'; Torquemada's ideas are ultimately quite similar to the conventionalized philanthropy which changes Christ's charity to calculated and socially fashionable beneficence. True compassion might be as infrequent in the reader's world as it is in Torquemada's.

The merger of these codes of meaning – the mundane and the divine, the material and the spiritual – into the larger processes of narration and signification assures the ultimate undecidability of their reading. The novella's capacity to be read as a parody of the exemplary genre and conventional morality, and as an exemplary moral statement in its own right, manifests an indeterminacy inherent in the interpretation of all narrative, even Scripture. It is this indeterminacy which Auerbach recognizes in his well-known essay, 'Figura', where he discusses the various concepts of prefiguration in biblical exegesis and the attempts to define its historical, literal, spiritual, or allegorical truth. Earlier notions of *figura* as a 'deeper meaning', 'deception', 'concealing', and even 'evasion' implicitly acknowledged the capacity of all discourse, of every word, to become figural when employed for poetic or rhetorical purposes.[13] A *figura* both is and is not what it seems at the same time; it pursues a meaning, only to evade it. The figure of Valentín functions in this way, for instance, by simultaneously implying a Christ-figure, parodying that implication, and assuming connotations of the Antichrist. The effect of this dynamics in the whole novella *Torquemada en hoguera* is to subvert any attempt by the reader at stabilizing its meanings or defining its terms. It is a text which demands constant re-interpretation because it ironizes all attempts at interpretation.

Conclusion

The preceding analysis of *Torquemada en la hoguera* indicates how that language which the reader recognizes as figural necessarily draws him into an endless process of interpretation and re-interpretation. In this study I have attempted to show how the novels of Benito Pérez Galdós foster the play of these indeterminable, and interminable, processes of reading. These processes, as they conceal and reveal meaning, effect irony. The reader participates in this irony through his awareness that another, deferred meaning contests the apparent one. And that other meaning may itself give way to another, opposing significance.

In the portraits of characters both their perceptions and often those of their society are shown to be superficial. The chapter entitled 'Navidad' in *La desheredada*, for example, reveals the distortion of other's attitudes as well as Isidora's. Isidora eats Christmas dinner alone with her brother in her room, immersed in her delusions of nobility. The scene also illustrates the hypocrisy and cruelty of Isidora's aunt, who prohibits her from joining in the Christmas festival. It reflects, too, on the society's – and perhaps even the reader's – materialistic pursuit of holiday shopping and feasting rather than the values of the religion whose founder it commemorates. The narrator observes:

Llegó Navidad, llegaron esos días de niebla y regocijo en que Madrid parece un manicomio suelto. Los hombres son atacados de una fiebre que se manifiesta en tres modos distintos: el delirio de la gula, la calentura de la lotería y el tétanos de las propinas. Todo lo que es espiritual, moral y delicado, todo lo que es del alma, huye o se eclipsa. La conmemoración más grande del mundo cristiano se celebra con el desencadenamiento de todos los apetitos. (IV. 1042)

In the description of settings, the initial perspective gives way to other, often contradictory ones. The detailed account of Nazarín's residence, for instance, first informs us that it is a 'casa de huéspedes', then 'el establecimiento hospitalario y benéfico de la *tía Chanfaina*'. Finally we are told: 'no tome nadie al pie de la letra lo de *casa de huéspedes* que al principio se ha dicho, pues entre las varias industrias de alojamiento que la *tía Chanfaina* ejercía en aquel rincón, y las del centro de Madrid, que todos hemos conocido en la edad estudiantil, y aun después de ella, no hay otra semejanza que la del nombre' (v. 1679). Even the narrator, the guiding 'voice of reading', is ultimately incorporated into the novel's continuum of linguistic play. These novels repeatedly give way to new meanings; in this manifestation of multiple ironies they define their own irony and that of interpretation in general: the claim to any objectivity at all.

Irony dissolves the security of objectivity; once we become aware that others lack that security, we recognize that we might, too. Galdós' novels break down the conventions of representational interpretation; they contrive to make of language a signifying process incapable of absolutely capturing any object but itself. Each interpretation or evaluation of a novel incurs another, contending one. Language bears a figural relationship to a reality which it confronts only in the fictions of the imagination. When metaphor pretends to comprehend a meaning beyond its own system of language, it becomes ironic; by claiming to apprehend an object beyond itself, it marks its own limitations. When we believe that language conveys authentic, absolute reality, we become victims of the intrinsic irony of language. When we believe that our interpretation is 'correct', the narrative invites yet another meaning.

Hayden White has discussed in *Metahistory* the movement in nineteenth-century thought from a search for metaphorical approximations of reality to the recognition that no perspective on reality is 'broader' than another. This recognition led to an awareness that all approximations were inevitably ironic because they were liable to displacement by the next, equally valid, but opposing interpretation. He writes (p. 37) of the literature – histories, philosophies of history, and novels – which recognized and assumed the ironic mode:

Irony is in one sense metatropological, for it is deployed in the self-conscious awareness of the possible misuse of figurative language. Irony presupposes the occupation of a 'realistic' perspective on reality, from which a nonfigurative representation of the world of experience might be provided. Irony thus represents a stage of consciousness in which the problematical nature of language itself has become recognized. It points to the potential foolishness of all linguistic characterizations of reality as much as to the absurdity of the beliefs it parodies. It is therefore 'dialectical', as Kenneth Burke has noted, though not so much in its apprehension of the process of the world as in its apprehension of the capacity of language to obscure more than it clarifies in any act of verbal figuration. In Irony, figurative language folds back upon itself and brings its own potentialities for distorting perception under question.

Galdós' novels manifest this process of language's folding back upon itself, and the reader experiences this same process as he becomes aware of it. This self-reflective criticism comprehends other realms of the reader's experience, besides the reading of novels.

Irony serves to destroy the notion of a 'final reading'. This is especially so in Galdós' later novels, where there are no definite resolutions to the questions posed. Many characters from the later novels of the *serie contemporánea* do not return to a conventional society; they are not re-integrated into the novelistic system. This disassociation perhaps begins with Fortunata, who achieves her ideal, unlike Máximo Manso or Isidora Rufete before her. Fortunata's illegitimate son does become the heir to his father's 'dynasty' in *Fortunata y Jacinta*. Still, in this novel, she can achieve this goal only through her death. Fortunata manages to transcend social structure – and its ironic claim to be 'morally right' – only by leaving it. In some later novels, however, the characters do not have to die in order to achieve their ideals. Nazarín is finally allowed to continue his Christ-like sacrifice, but he is branded insane by most of his society. His story thus ends in the ambiguity with which it began. Nazarín does not renounce his illusion, as Don Quijote did, nor does the narrator judge him, as happens with Isidora and Rosalía. This movement from social integration to disassociation in Galdós' later novels is the inverse of that in Cervantes' last works – especially *Don Quijote* Part II and the *Persiles* – whose characters return to acceptance of social and religious convention. Only Benina, in *Misericordia*, seems to overcome irony while remaining in the world. Though a social outcast, she is not labeled insane. *Misericordia* suggests that transcendence of irony is possible, but only through an acceptance of the inevitable coexistence of opposites in the world. Benina accepts each event – even banishment from the family she faithfully served – and each attitude – even ingratitude – as equally valid. Benina solves the dilemma faced by all those characters in Galdós' works who could not integrate their own subjective points of view with those of others, nor realize that theirs were not absolute. She resigns herself to accepting hunger, poverty, and selfishness as inherent conditions of the world.

Galdós' novels reveal the subjectivity of both the individual and collective social opinion. Even the most generally accepted, so-called objective, and moral opinion is shown to be as relative as the most blind, insane, or selfish individual prejudice. While the reader may condemn the illusions of Isidora and Rosalía or the materialism of Torquemada, the narrative shows that they are only single instances of delusions at work in the novelistic society as a whole. This society is often associated very closely with the reader's own. We come to see the deceptions – mistaken or purposeful – perpetrated by Máximo Manso, José María Bueno de Guzmán, or Manuel Infante as they propose their sincere, reasoned interpretations of themselves and the world; we may also suddenly become aware of our own faulty interpretations. Like those characters, we may be misreaders of our own capacities for insight. One character's *quijotismo* is another's truth, the play of *loco* and *cuerdo* originally illustrated in *Don Quijote*. As the narrator observes in *La desheredada*, Leganés is defined only by its arbitrarily set walls. We conventionally assume that language describes reality, even though it is only an arbitrary system. Galdós' novels continually demonstrate – through the illusions of character, narrator, and reader, and through the destruction of the conventions of interpretation – that absolute objectivity is impossible; *imagen* cannot be equated with *vida*, nor language with reality. By means of the 'realism' which necessarily bears an ironic relation to reality, the novels of Galdós ultimately destroy the pretense of representational meaning.

The novels of the *serie contemporánea* continually demonstrate how irony makes victims of the observer, or reader, as well as of the observed, or narrative. While the reader complacently considers the folly of Isidora, for example, he may neglect his own. But the narrative can suddenly make the reader realize that irony has extended beyond the printed page to include him. The abrupt movement from history to discourse, the use of the free indirect style, or any one of the conventions which assume the reader's compliance, can make him aware of his incorporation into the novelistic system of ironies. The reader must then re-evaluate all the levels in the process of interpretation itself. When the novel seems to be revealing the most obvious ironies, the reader must be most alert to the possible irony of his own position. For example, when the narrator declares that Torquemada was *sin duda* morally weak as he ran from Valentín's bedroom, it is presumed that the reader agrees. But if he agrees too quickly he will eventually have to apply that criticism of Torquemada to his own society, whose values

may appear very similar. Muecke discusses (p. 229) how the ironist –
he who creates or views another's irony, either as writer or reader – is
also a victim:

What the ironist objectively sees, is, to put it in the most basic terms, a
soulless slave mechanically performing meaningless acts in a meaningless
world while being confidently unaware that he is anything but a rational
self-determining person behaving purposefully in a meaningful world.
This induces in the ironist the feeling that he is everything that the victim
is not. But the situation the ironist feels and assumes himself to be in is
precisely the same situation as the victim mistakenly assumes that *he* is in.
The only difference is that the ironist is looking at a victim; the result,
however, of his focusing his attention in this direction is that he leaves his
rear exposed.

This is certainly true of the reader of Galdós, who is never more insecure
in his position than when he recognizes the acuity of Galdosian irony.

The archetypal victim of irony is man, and the archetypal ironist is
God. This relationship is allegorized in *El amigo Manso* when Manso
finally recognizes his insignificance as he gazes from the clouds. Benina
also sees from the slums of Madrid that all persons are equal, regardless
of money or appearance, that there will always be material inequities,
and that each perspective on the world is as valid as the next. Irony
allows a temporary escape from the feeling of insignificance and subjectivity because it allows a certain skepticism and distance from the
'inferior' victim. Nonetheless, in Galdós' novels we are continually
made aware of the possibility of our own irony while we are observing
it in others. The novel, as language, establishes its own irony. 'Ironic
detachment', like objectivity and realism, is only one more perspective.
Still, irony may be the only way to deal with life, short of suicide or
insanity, once the ironic nature of the world is recognized. The description of the church of San Sebastián displays the ironic stance which
Benina adopts in the placid acceptance of life's – of Madrid's – *eterna
guasa*. Irony becomes a way of viewing, while continually re-evaluating,
the world and oneself. Hayden White writes (pp. 37–8) that:

The trope of Irony, then, provides a linguistic paradigm of a mode of
thought which is radically self-critical with respect not only to a given
characterization of the world of experience but also to the very effort to
capture adequately the truth of things in language. It is, in short, a model
of the linguistic protocol in which skepticism in thought and relativism in
ethics are conventionally expressed.
Existentially projected into a full-blown world view, Irony would
appear to be transideological. Irony can be used *tactically* for defense of

either Liberal or Conservative ideological positions, depending on whether the Ironist is speaking against established social forms or against 'utopian' reformers seeking to change the status quo. And it can be used offensively by the Anarchist and the Radical, to pillory the ideals of their Liberal and Conservative opponents. But, as the basis of a world view, Irony tends to dissolve all belief in the possibility of positive political actions. In its apprehension of the essential folly or absurdity of the human condition, it tends to engender belief in the 'madness' of civilization itself and to inspire a Mandarin-like disdain for those seeking to grasp the nature of social reality in either science or art.

Such a picture of the folly of civilization is fully projected in one of Galdós' last novels, *El caballero encantado* (*Cuento real . . . inverosímil*), published in 1909. Here *la Madre*, the history of Spain, takes the hero on a fantastic journey which surveys the country's decadence at the turn of the century. The last series of the *Episodios nacionales*, Galdós' historical novels, also become fantastic, skeptical visions of civilization and history. The progression that Hayden White describes in historical literature from the metaphorical to the ironic mode might be observed in the progressive development of Galdós' *Episodios* from the first series to the last, as well as in his contemporary novels.

If we were to view Galdós' work as the creation of a global ironic vision, it would mitigate much of the insolvable controversy aroused by those seeking to categorize his political sympathies. The identifications of Galdós as a liberal, a conservative, or a political hypocrite have all been equally well 'proven' by the proponents of these classifications. Yet no one social, political, or religious group was exempt from his irony, or from his sympathy. I have attempted to show how codes of irony traverse Galdós' novels from the level of a single word, through the development of character and theme, to the process of reading. Many ironies – perhaps the most obvious – have been left unmentioned. There are general dramatic ironies, such as 'pride comes before the fall' (illustrated by Isidora, for example); or there are ironically opposed characters, such as Fortunata and Jacinta. As in the case of *Fortunata y Jacinta*, the titles of the novels often define the ironies they embrace. By identifying one sense of a novel, they ironically imply the other; *La desheredada* is not the story of a disinherited girl, but only of one who thought she was; *El doctor Centeno* refers to the urchin Centeno, who is not a doctor, nor even the main character of the story. *Realidad* is a fantastic tale. The title *Ángel Guerra* is a quasi-oxymoron, which defines the irony of the protagonist's quest. Subtitles and chapter headings offer many other inverted meanings, as do the names of characters. The novels of Benito Pérez Galdós continually proffer irony; they begin and end in it through their insistent juxtaposition of contrary elements. Their ultimate irony, however, resides in the conventional gesture by which we render complementary the irreducibly contrary realms of language and reality.

Notes

Introduction

1 *Anatomy of Criticism: Four Essays*, Princeton Paperback edn (Princeton Univ. Press, 1971), p. 41.
2 This is the simplest definition of the rhetorical figure of irony. Richard A. Lanham, *A Handlist of Rhetorical Terms* (Berkeley and Los Angeles: Univ. of California Press, 1969), p. 61: 'expressing a meaning directly opposite to that intended'.
3 See Lukács, *The Theory of the Novel*, trans. Anna Bostock (Cambridge: Massachusetts Institute of Technology Press, 1971), esp. pp. 75–93; Frye, esp. pp. 35–43 and 176–239; Booth, *A Rhetoric of Irony* (Chicago and London: Univ. of Chicago Press, 1975), esp. ch. 1, 'Stable Irony', pp. 1–31.
4 Robert Scholes and Robert Kellogg, *The Nature of Narrative* (London and New York: Oxford Univ. Press, 1966), p. 240.
5 London: Methuen, 1969, p. 3.
6 In *The Georgia Review*, 29 (1975), 42–60.
7 *Structuralist Poetics: Structuralism, Linguistics, and the Study of Literature* (Ithaca: Cornell Univ. Press, 1975),p. 139.
8 *Flaubert. The Uses of Uncertainty* (Ithaca: Cornell Univ. Press, 1975), p. 24.

1 The irony of portrait

1 *S/Z*, trans. Richard Miller (New York: Hill and Wang, 1974), p. 67.
2 Gustavo Correa treats this confrontation between fiction and reality in *La desheredada* in *Realidad, ficción y símbolo en las novelas de Pérez Galdós: ensayo de estética realista* (Bogotá: Instituto Caro y Cuervo, 1967), pp. 65–74.
3 *La desheredada* was first published as a *folletín* or serial novel.
4 Wolfgang Iser, *The Implied Reader: Patterns of Communication in Prose Fiction from Bunyan to Beckett* (Baltimore: The Johns Hopkins Univ. Press, 1974), pp. xi–xiv.
5 I quote from Benito Pérez Galdós, *Obras completas*, ed. Federico Carlos Sainz de Robles, 6th edn (Madrid: Aguilar, 1966); the volume and page numbers will be given thus: iv. 966.
6 For an extended discussion of the reader's appropriation of novelistic decisions, see Booth, pp. 39–43, and Iser, p. 108.
7 For detailed historical analyses and working definitions of the free indirect style, or free indirect speech as it is also called, see: Roy Pascal, *The Dual Voice* (Manchester Univ. Press, 1977); Guillermo Verdín Díaz, *Introducción al estilo indirecto libre en español*, Revista de Filología Española, *Anejo* 91 (Madrid: Real Academia Española, 1970), and also Stephen Ullman's dis-

cussion of it in *Style in the French Novel* (Cambridge Univ. Press, 1957), esp. pp. 99–120.

8 The influence of naturalism in this novel contributes to the ambiguity of Isidora's mental state; she has a family history of neuroses, but does not display any explicit illnesses herself. The Marquesa summarizes the ambiguity by calling her 'impostura o demente'. For discussions of naturalism in *La desheredada*, see: Eamonn Rodgers, 'Galdós' *La desheredada* and naturalism'. *Bulletin of Hispanic Studies*, 45 (1968), 285–98; Carlos Rovetta, 'El naturalismo de Galdós en *La desheredada*', *Nosotros*, 2nd series, 84 (1943), 275–84.

9 Verdín Díaz, p. 125, and Maria Helena de Novais Paiva, *Contribução para uma estilística da ironia*, Publicações do Centro de Estudos Filológicos (Lisbon, 1971), p. 201; both discuss the subjective view permitted to the reader through the free indirect style.

10 In addition, anastrophe, hysteron proteron, and other forms of hyperbaton in general create such 'extravagance'. This 'deviant' or 'unusual' use of language suggests the Formalists' 'de-familiarization'.

11 The use of the historical chronicle will be discussed more fully in Chapter 3.

12 Pascal, pp. 84–5, discusses the intrusive effect in *Middlemarch* of the narrator's sophistications juxtaposed to the character's ignorance.

13 Enrique Tierno Galván, 'Aparición y desarrollo de nuevas perspectivas de valoración social en el siglo XIX: lo cursi', *Revista de Estudios Políticos*, 42 (1952), 85–106.

14 This reference recalls the fact that each time Isidora prays it is for utterly selfish and vain reasons.

15 *S/Z*, section XX, 'The dissolve of voices', pp. 41–2.

16 An especially perceptive article on Rosalía is Jennifer Lowe, 'Galdós' presentation of Rosalía in *La de Bringas*', *Hispanófila*, 50 (1974), 49–65.

17 For a discussion of satire versus irony, see: Muecke, pp. 23–9, in the section 'The Duality of Irony', and Ronald Paulson, ed., *Satire: Essays in Criticism* (N.J.: Prentice-Hall, 1971), esp. pp. 340–9 of his article 'The Fictions of Satire', where he discusses why satire is a didactic mode.

18 Roland Barthes, 'L'effet du réel', *Communications*, 11 (1968), 84–9.

19 Paulson, 'The Fictions of Satire', in *Satire*, pp. 340–9, discusses the distancing effect of satire.

20 Ullman, *Style in the French Novel*, esp. pp. 94–7, discusses the use of the imperfect tense in the free indirect style. Verdín Díaz, p. 129, also notes this. The function of Benveniste's distinction between *histoire* and *discours* will be discussed at greater length in Chapter 4.

21 For Galdós' ironic portrayal of Pez, see ch. XII of *La desheredada*, Part I, 'Los peces (sermón)'.

22 Verdín Díaz, 91ff., identifies question and exclamation as the most frequent functions of the free indirect style.

23 'Criteria for Style Analysis', *Word*, 15 (1959), 154–74.

24 Ullman, *Style in the French Novel*, p. 160. See also his *Language and Style* (Oxford: Basil Blackwell, 1964), pp. 100–11.

25 Barthes, *S/Z*, p. 90, discusses how narrative is not a hierarchy of meaning or 'nesting narratives' or 'a narrative within the narrative': 'Since narrative is both merchandise and the relation of the contract of which it is the object, there can no longer be any question of setting up a rhetorical hierarchy between the two parts of the tale, as is the common practice.'

26 On the Refugio–Rosalía scene, see: William H. Shoemaker, 'Galdós's

Classical Scene in *La de Bringas*', *Hispanic Review*, 27 (1959), 423–34; Julian Palley, 'Aspectos de *La de Bringas*', *Kentucky Romance Quarterly*, 16 (1969), 339–48.

2   The setting of irony

1 Ullman in *Style in the French Novel* discusses the crescendo effect of linguistic inversion, especially in ch. IV, section ii, where he analyzes Hugo's ironic use of inversion. Generally, he says, 'when there is a discrepancy between the impressive *crescendo* structure and the mediocrity of the subject, the effect is one of ironical anticlimax' (p. 158). See also his *Language and Style*, pp. 109–11, for a similar discussion.

2 Ullman, *Style in the French Novel*, ch. IV, discusses Flaubert's impressionistic techniques and how word order can reflect the images as they reach the perceiver (pp. 164ff.); also see his discussion of the Goncourts' use of impressionistic techniques, especially for pictorial and visual effects (pp. 167–73).

3 Geraldine M. Scanlon discusses the materialistic permeation of all the characters in the Torquemada series, even San Pedro to a certain extent, in 'Torquemada: "Becerro de oro"', *Modern Language Notes*, 91 (1976), 264–76.

4 There are two doctoral dissertations which deal extensively with the Cervantine influence in Galdós' works, giving particular attention to that in *Nazarín*: J. C. Herman, 'Don Quijote and the Novels of Pérez Galdós' (University of Kansas, 1950); and Betty Jean Zeidner, 'Cervantine Aspects of the Novelistic Art of Benito Pérez Galdós' (University of California, 1957).

5 There has been much controversy over Nazarín's role as either a Christ figure or a quixotic character, especially in articles from *Anales Galdosianos*, 2 (1967): Ciriaco Morón Arroyo, '*Nazarín y Halma*: sentido y unidad', 67–81; Frank P. Bowman, 'On the Definition of Jesus in Modern Fiction', 53–66; Alexander A. Parker, '*Nazarín*, or the Passion of Our Lord Jesus Christ according to Galdós', 81–101. In a more recent issue, *Anales Galdosianos*, 9 (1974), much of the controversy seems to have been resolved and attention is more appropriately turned to questions of the reader's role in interpreting Nazarín: Antonio Ramos Gascón, 'Presentación', 79–80; John W. Kronik, 'Estructura dinámica en *Nazarín*', 81–98; Peter B. Goldman, 'Galdós and the Aesthetic of Ambiguity: Notes on the Thematic Structure of *Nazarín*', 99–112; and Brian J. Dendle, 'Point of View in *Nazarín*: An Appendix to Goldman', 113–23, who writes: 'It is we, the reader, who must finally define saintliness or madness; it is we, the reader, who must come to terms with Nazarín and with Christ Himself; Galdós, ironically, refuses any resolution of the problems he has so skilfully posed.'

6 'The Christ Figure in *Misericordia*', *Anales Galdosianos*, 2 (1967), 103–30.

7 Robert Kirsner, 'La ironía del bien en *Misericordia*', *Actas del tercer congreso internacional de hispanistas* (Mexico: El Colegio de México, 1970), pp. 495–9.

8 After completing this chapter I became aware of a recent article on setting in Galdós: William R. Risley, 'Setting in the Galdós Novel, 1881–1885', *Hispanic Review*, 46 (1978), 23–40. He traces Galdós' development of setting in the *Novelas contemporáneas* through the ratio of interior to exterior settings. He finds that Galdós moves from unique to more common settings and from broad geographical scenes to an almost exclusive use of interiors, and

says these changes reflect 'that Galdós is concentrating upon a deeper portrayal of more intimate human relations and of the psychological inner life'
(p. 32).

3 The narrator of irony

1 See p. 17 of this study for a discussion of the episode.
2 See Ruth El Saffar, *Distance and Control in 'Don Quixote': A Study of
   Narrative Technique*, North Carolina Studies in the Romance Languages and
   Literatures, 147 (Chapel Hill: Univ. of N. Carolina Press, 1975).
3 See note 24 in ch. 1.
4 Raymond S. Willis, Jr, *The Phantom Chapters of the Quijote* (New York:
   Hispanic Institute, 1953).
5 On the character–narrator of *La de Bringas* see P. A. Bly, 'The Use of
   Distance in Galdós's *La de Bringas*', *Modern Language Review*, 69 (1974),
   87–99.
6 William H. Shoemaker, 'Galdós's Literary Creativity: Don José Ido del
   Sagrario', *Hispanic Review*, 19 (1951), 204–37.
7 Gustavo Correa studies these two characters in *Realidad, ficción y símbolo*,
   ch. VII, 'Dos héroes de ficción', pp. 100–15.
8 See, for example, Ricardo Gullón, 'La invención del personaje en *El amigo
   Manso*', *Ínsula*, 148 (1959), 1–2, and his '*El amigo Manso* entre Galdós y
   Unamuno', *Mundo Nuevo*, 4 (Oct. 1966), 32–9; see also his '*El amigo
   Manso*, nivola galdosiana', in *Técnicas de Galdós* (Madrid: Taurus, 1970),
   pp. 59–102; Eamonn Rodgers, 'Realismo y mito en *El amigo Manso*',
   Cuadernos Hispanoamericanos, 250–2 (1970–1), 430–44.
9 This concept is not unlike Shklovsky's 'de-personalization'.
10 Miguel de Cervantes, *Don Quijote de la Mancha*, Part I, in *Obras completas*,
   ed. Ángel Valbuena Prat, 16th edn (Madrid: Aguilar, 1970), p. 1252.
11 Miguel de Cervantes, *Los trabajos de Persiles y Sigismunda*, in *Obras
   completas*, p. 1915.
12 '*El amigo Manso* and the Relativity of Reality', *Revista de Estudios
   Hispánicos*, 7 (1973), 113–25.
13 Sherman Eoff, 'A Galdosian Version of The Picaresque Psychology', *Modern
   Language Forum*, 38 (1953), 1–12.
14 Francisco Rico, ed., *La novela picaresca española*, 2nd edn (Barcelona:
   Editorial Planeta, 1970). In a lengthy introduction, Rico outlines the problematic reconciliation of the sinner–actor and the repentant author in the
   Guzmán. See especially section ii, 'Atalaya de la vida humana', pp. cvii–cli.
15 On José María as a hero, see his comments in Part II, ch. XXII, and Arthur
   Terry, '*Lo prohibido*: Unreliable Narrator and Untruthful Narrative', in
   Galdós Studies I, ed. J. E. Varey (London: Támesis, 1970), 62–89.
16 Pascal, p. 68, states that the use of the free indirect style by a first-person
   narrator is rare, and often contrary to the spirit of the story. Its use in *Lo
   prohibido* is another of the narrative's contradictions.
17 *Metahistory: The Historical Imagination in Nineteenth-Century Europe*
   (Baltimore and London: The Johns Hopkins Univ. Press, 1975), p. 37.
18 For example, see Correa's reading of them in his *Realidad, ficción y símbolo*,
   ch. IX, 'La interpretación de la realidad', pp. 145–62.
19 'El tópico, fenómeno sociológico', *Revista de Estudios Políticos*, 45–6 (1952),
   111–31.
20 See Iser's explanation of expectation and retrospection in *The Implied*

Reader, especially the last chapter, 'A phenomenological approach to reading'.

21 Joaquín Gimeno Casalduero, 'El tópico en la obra de Pérez Galdós', *Boletín del Seminario de Derecho Político*, 8–9 (Salamanca, 1956), 35–52.

22 John Sinnigen, 'Resistance and Rebellion in *Tristana*', *Modern Language Notes*, 91 (1976), 277–91, and Gonzalo Sobejano, 'Galdós y el vocabulario de los amantes', *Anales Galdosianos*, 1 (1966), 85–100, discuss this aspect of *Tristana*.

23 See notes 19 and 21 above and E. Tierno Galván, 'Notas sobre la tertulia', *Boletín del Seminario de Derecho Político*, 8–9 (Salamanca, 1956), 17–34.

24 This is Iser's thesis, which is basically congruent with Culler's concept of the conventions of reading, which I believe is ironic when the reader contradicts himself.

25 'Forma literaria y sensibilidad social en *La incógnita* y *Realidad* de Galdós', *Revista Hispánica Moderna*, 30 (1964), 89–107.

26 Leopoldo Alas (Clarín), *Galdós* (Madrid: Renacimiento, 1912), pp. 200–1.

4 The texture of irony

1 Nicholas G. Round observes in 'Time and Torquemada: Three Notes on Galdosian Chronology', *Anales Galdosianos*, 6 (1971), 79–97: 'Writing on 16th April 1889 to the Catalan novelist Narciso Oller, who had just congratulated him on his success in this novel *Torquemada en la hoguera*, Galdós described the story as "escrito a la carrera y casi por compromiso." That a work so composed could incorporate technical features as sophisticated as that analysed here is striking evidence of the sureness and subtlety of Galdós' novelistic instinct.' He quotes from W. H. Shoemaker, *Una amistad literaria: la correspondencia epistolar entre Galdós y Narciso Oller* (Barcelona, 1964), p. 44.

2 Miguel de Cervantes, *Las novelas ejemplares*, in *Obras completas*, p. 924.

3 See pp. 29, 31 on the details of description in Rosalía's portrait.

4 Emil Benveniste, *Problems in General Linguistics*, trans. Mary E. Meek (Univ. of Miami Press, 1971), chs. xviii–xx, discusses these categories.

5 *Ibid.*, esp. ch. xviii, 'Relationships of Person in the Verb'.

6 Boris Tomaschevsky, 'Thematics', in *Russian Formalist Criticism*, ed. and trans. L. T. Lemon and M. J. Reis (Lincoln: Univ. of Nebraska Press, 1965), p. 95.

7 Matías Montes Huidobro, *XIX: Superficie y fondo del estilo*, Estudios de Hispanófila, 17 (Chapel Hill: Univ. of N. Carolina Dept. of Romance Languages and Literatures, 1971), p. 45.

8 'En toda la extensión de la palabra' is a *muletilla* of Doña Lupe in *Fortunata y Jacinta*, where she is Torquemada's cohort.

9 See my comments on 'sin duda' on p. 16.

10 See p. 17 of this study for a discussion of the corresponding episode in *La desheredada*.

11 See Scanlon, 'Torquemada: "Becerro de oro"'.

12 Compare with Matthew xiv, 45–6: 'Again, the kingdom of heaven is like a merchant in search of fine pearls, who, on finding one pearl of great value, went and sold all that he had and bought it.' *Torquemada en la hoguera* employs an ironic inversion of this text.

13 Erich Auerbach, 'Figura', in *Scenes from the Drama of European Literature: Six Essays* (New York: Meridian Books, 1959), pp. 11–76.

Bibliography

The following bibliography lists only those works cited in the notes to the text. For further bibliography, the reader should consult Hensley C. Woodbridge, *Benito Pérez Galdós: A Selective Annotated Bibliography* (Metuchen, N.J.: The Scarecrow Press, 1975).

Alas, Leopoldo (Clarín). *Galdós.* Madrid: Renacimiento, 1912

Alter, Robert. 'History and Imagination in the 19th Century Novel'. *Georgia Review*, 29 (1975), 42–60

Auerbach, Erich. 'Figura', in *Scenes from the Drama of European Literature: Six Essays.* New York: Meridian Books, 1959, pp. 11–76

Barthes, Roland. 'L'effet du réel', *Communications*, 11 (1968), 84–9
   S/Z. Trans. Richard Miller. New York: Hill and Wang, 1974

Benveniste, Emile. *Problems in General Linguistics.* Trans. Mary Elizabeth Meek. University of Miami Press, 1971

Bly, P. A. 'The Use of Distance in Galdós's *La de Bringas*', *Modern Language Review*, 69 (1974), 87–99

Booth, Wayne C. *A Rhetoric of Irony.* Chicago and London: University of Chicago Press, 1975

Bowman, Frank P. 'On the Definition of Jesus in Modern Fiction', *Anales Galdosianos*, 2 (1967), 53–66

Cervantes Saavedra, Miguel de. *Obras completas.* Ed. Ángel Valbuena Prat. 16th edn. Madrid: Aguilar, 1970

Correa, Gustavo. *Realidad, ficción y símbolo en las novelas de Pérez Galdós: ensayo de estética realista.* Bogotá: Instituto Caro y Cuervo, 1967

Culler, Jonathan. *Flaubert: The Uses of Uncertainty.* Ithaca: Cornell University Press, 1975.
   Structuralist Poetics: Structuralism, Linguistics, and the Study of Literature. Ithaca: Cornell University Press, 1975.

Dendle, Brian J. 'Point of View in *Nazarín:* An Appendix to Goldman'. *Anales Galdosianos*, 9 (1974), 113–23.

El Saffar, Ruth Snodgrass. *Distance and Control in 'Don Quixote': A Study of Narrative Technique.* North Carolina Studies in the Romance Languages and Literatures, 147. Chapel Hill: University of North Carolina Press, 1975

Eoff, Sherman. 'A Galdosian Version of the Picaresque Psychology', *Modern Language Forum*, 38 (1953), 1–12

Frye, Northrop. *Anatomy of Criticism: Four Essays.* Princeton paperback edn. Princeton University Press, 1971

Gimeno Casalduero, Joaquín. 'El tópico en la obra de Pérez Galdós', *Boletín del Seminario de Derecho Político*, 8–9 (Salamanca, 1956), 35–52

Goldman, Peter B. 'Galdós and the Aesthetic of Ambiguity: Notes on the Thematic Structure of *Nazarín*', *Anales Galdosianos*, 9 (1974), 99–112

Gullón, Ricardo. '*El amigo Manso* entre Galdós y Unamuno', *Mundo Nuevo*, 4 (Oct. 1966), 32–9

'La invención del personaje en *El amigo Manso*', *Ínsula*, 148 (1959), 1–2

Técnicas de Galdós. Madrid: Taurus, 1970.

Herman, J. C. 'Don Quijote and the Novels of Pérez Galdós', Doctoral diss. University of Kansas, 1950 (203 leaves)

Iser, Wolfgang. *The Implied Reader: Patterns of Communication in Prose Fiction from Bunyan to Beckett*. Baltimore: The Johns Hopkins University Press, 1974

Kirsner, Robert. 'La ironía del bien en *Misericordia*', in *Actas del tercer congreso internacional de hispanistas*, ed. C. H. Magis, pp. 495–9. Mexico: El Colegio de México, 1970

Kronik, John W. 'Estructura dinámica en *Nazarín*', *Anales Galdosianos*, 9 (1974), 81–98

Lanham, Richard A. *A Handlist of Rhetorical Terms*. Berkeley and Los Angeles, University of California Press, 1969

Lowe, Jennifer. 'Galdós' Presentation of Rosalía in *La de Bringas*', *Hispanófila*, 50 (1974), 49–65

Lukács, György. *The Theory of the Novel: A Historico-Philosophical Essay on the Forms of Great Epic Literature*. Trans. Anna Bostock. Cambridge: Massachusetts Institute of Technology Press, 1971

Montes Huidobro, Matías. *XIX: Superficie y fondo del estilo*. Estudios de Hispanófila, 17. Chapel Hill: University of North Carolina Department of Romance Languages, 1971

Morón Arroyo, Ciriaco. '*Nazarín y Halma*: sentido y unidad', *Anales Galdosianos*, 2 (1967), 67–81

Muecke, D. C. *The Compass of Irony*. London: Methuen, 1969.

Newton, Nancy. '*El amigo Manso* and the Relativity of Reality', *Revista de Estudios Hispánicos*, 7 (1973), 113–25.

Nimetz, Michael. *Humor in Galdós: A Study of the 'Novelas contemporáneas'*, New Haven and London: Yale University Press, 1968.

Novais Paiva, Maria Helena de. *Contribução para uma estilística da ironia*. Publicações do Centro de Estudos Filológicos. Lisbon, 1961

Palley, Julian. 'Aspectos de *La de Bringas*', *Kentucky Romance Quarterly*, 16 (1969), 339–48

Parker, Alexander A. '*Nazarín*, or the Passion of Our Lord Jesus Christ according to Galdós', *Anales Galdosianos*, 2 (1967), 81–101

Pascal, Roy. *The Dual Voice*. Manchester University Press, 1977

Paulson, Ronald, ed. *Satire: Essays in Criticism*. N.J.: Prentice-Hall, 1971

Pérez Galdós, Benito. *Obras completas*. Ed. Federico Carlos Sainz de Robles. 6th edn. 6 vols. Madrid: Aguilar, 1966

Ramos Gascón, Antonio. 'Presentación', *Anales Galdosianos*, 9 (1974), 79–80

Rico, Francisco, ed. *La novela picaresca española*. 2nd edn. Barcelona: Editorial Planeta, 1970

Riffaterre, Michael. 'Criteria for Style Analysis', *Word*, 15 (1959), 154–74

Risley, William R. 'Setting in the Galdós Novel, 1881–1885', *Hispanic Review*, 46 (1978), 23–40

Rodgers, Eamonn. 'Galdós' *La desheredada* and naturalism', *Bulletin of Hispanic Studies*, 45 (1968), 285–98

'Realismo y mito en *El amigo Manso*', *Cuadernos Hispano-americanos*, 250–2 (1970–1), 430–44

Round, Nicholas G. 'Time and Torquemada: Three Notes on Galdosian Chronology', *Anales Galdosianos*, 6 (1971), 79–97

Rovetta, Carlos. 'El naturalismo de Galdós en *La desheredada*', *Nosotros*, 2nd series, 84 (1943), 275–84

Russell, Robert, 'The Christ Figure in *Misericordia*', *Anales Galdosianos*, 2 (1967), 103–30

Scanlon, Geraldine M. 'Torquemada: "Becerro de oro"', *Modern Language Notes*, 91 (1976), 264–76

Scholes, Robert, and Kellogg, Robert. *The Nature of Narrative*. London and New York: Oxford University Press, 1966

Shoemaker, William H. 'Galdós's Classical Scene in *La de Bringas*', *Hispanic Review*, 27 (1959), 423–34

'Galdós's Literary Creativity: Don José Ido del Sagrario', *Hispanic Review*, 19 (1951), 204–37

Sinnigen, John. 'Resistance and Rebellion in *Tristana*', *Modern Language Notes*, 91 (1976), 277–91

Sobejano, Gonzalo. 'Forma literaria y sensibilidad social en *La incógnita* y *Realidad* de Galdós', *Revista Hispánica Moderna*, 30 (1964), 89–107

'Galdós y el vocabulario de los amantes', *Anales Galdosianos*, 1 (1966), 85–100

Terry, Arthur. '*Lo prohibido*: Unreliable Narrator and Untruthful Narrative', in *Galdós Studies I*, ed. J. E. Varey. London: Támesis, 1970, pp. 62–89.

Tierno Galván, Enrique. 'Aparición y desarrollo de nuevas perspectivas de valoración social en el siglo XIX: lo cursi', *Revista de Estudios Políticos*, 42 (1952), 85–106

'El tópico: fenómeno sociológico', *Revista de Estudios Políticos*, 45–6 (1952), 111–31.

'Notas sobre la tertulia', *Boletín del Seminario de Derecho Político*, 8–9 (Salamanca, 1956), 17–34

Tomaschevsky, Boris. 'Thematics', in *Russian Formalist Criticism*. Ed. and trans. L. T. Lemon and M. J. Reis, pp. 61–95. Lincoln: University of Nebraska Press, 1965

Ullman, Stephen. *Language and Style*. Oxford: Basil Blackwell, 1964
Style in the French Novel. Cambridge University Press, 1957

Verdín Díaz, Guillermo. *Introducción al estilo indirecto libre en español*. Revista de Filología Española *Anejo* 91. Madrid: Real Academia Española, 1970

White, Hayden. *Metahistory: The Historical Imagination in Nineteenth-Century Europe*. Baltimore and London: The Johns Hopkins University Press, paperback edn, 1975

Willis, Raymond S., Jr. *The Phantom Chapters of the Quijote*. New York: Hispanic Institute, 1953.

Zeidner, Betty Jean. 'Cervantine Aspects of the Novelistic Art of Benito Pérez Galdós', Doctoral diss. University of California, 1957 (230 leaves)

Index

Alas, Leopoldo (Clarín), 28, 90, 93
Alemán, Mateo, *Guzmán de Alfarache*, 75
Alter, Robert, 2
Auerbach, Erich, 120–1

Balzac, Honoré de, 1
Barthes, Roland, 5, 26, 64, 130 nn.18 and 25
Benveniste, Emile, 99, 130 n.20
Bible, 58, 105, 106–7, 119–20, 133 n.12
Bly, P. A., 132 n.6
Booth, Wayne, 3, 7, 129 n.3
Bowman, Frank P., 131 n.5

Cervantes, Miguel de
Don Quijote, 2, 6, 14, 26, 44, 46, 59, 65–70, 74, 77, 124–5; chronicle device in, 17, 57, 58, 66, 116; 'El curioso impertinente', 81; phantom chapters, 67–9; tragicomedy, 58, 93
Los trabajos de Persiles y Sigismunda, 124, 132 n.11
Novelas ejemplares, 96
Correa, Gustavo, 129 n.2 to Chapter 1, 132 nn.7 and 18
Culler, Jonathan, 3, 4, 64, 133 n.24

Dendle, Brian J., 131 n.5
Dostoevsky, Feodor, 75

El Saffar, Ruth, 132 n.2
Eliot, George, *Middlemarch*, 130 n.12
Eoff, Sherman, 75

Fielding, Henry, *Tom Jones*, 100
Flaubert, Gustave, 1, 30, 131 n.2
Frye, Northrop, 1

Gimeno Casalduero, Joaquín, 85–6
Goldman, Peter B., 131 n.5
Goncourt, Edmond de and Jules de, 131 n.2
Gullón, Ricardo, 132 n.8

Herman, J. C., 131 n.4
Hugo, Victor, 131 n.1

Iser, Wolfgang, 4, 7, 81, 87–9, 98, 132–3 n.20

Kellogg, Robert, 1
Kirsner, Robert, 63
Kronik, John W., 131 n.5

Lanham, Richard A., 129 n.1 to Introduction
Lowe, Jennifer, 130 n.16
Lukács, Gÿorgy, 3, 129 n.3 Introduction

Montes Huidobro, Matías, 103
Morón Arroyo, Ciriaco, 131 n.5
Muecke, D. C., 2, 4, 126, 130 n.17

Newton, Nancy, 74
Novais Paiva, Maria H. de, 130 n.9

Palley, Julian, 130–1 n.26
Parker, Alexander A., 131 n.5
Pascal, Roy, 9–10, 100–1, 109, 129–30 n.7, 130 n.12, 132 n.16
Paulson, Ronald, 130 nn.17 and 19
Pérez Galdós, Benito
Ángel Guerra, 48, 68–9, 127
Doña Perfecta, 48, 63
El abuelo, 87, 94
El amigo Manso, 31, 36, 70–5, 126
El caballero encantado, 63, 127
El doctor Centeno, 69, 87, 127
Episodios nacionales, 127
Fortunata y Jacinta, 48, 124, 127, 133 n.8
Gloria, 48
Halma, 67
La de Bringas, 28, 29, 30, 31, 32, 33–46, 48–52, 53, 68, 71, 87
La desheredada, 6–27, 28, 29, 32, 36, 38, 41, 65, 66, 67, 87, 114, 115, 122, 125, 130 n.21

Pérez Galdós, Benito (*cont.*)
  La incógnita, 79–87, 89, 92
  La loca de la casa, 94
  Lo prohibido, 48, 75–9
  Misericordia, 59–63, 67, 124
  Nazarín, 55–9, 66, 67, 122
  Realidad, 80, 81, 85, 87–94, 127
  Tormento, 28–33, 36, 38, 45, 68, 87
  Torquemada en la hoguera, 95–121, 122
  Torquemada y San Pedro, 52–5, 102, 119
  Tristana, 86
Proust, Marcel, 30

Ramos Gascón, Antonio, 131 n.5
Rico, Francisco, 132 n.14
Riffaterre, Michael, 130 n.23
Risley, William R., 131–2 n.8
Rodgers, Eamonn, 130 n.8, 132 n.8
Rojas, Fernando de, *La Celestina*, 87
Round, Nicholas G., 133 n.1
Rovetta, Carlos, 130 n.8
Russell, Robert, 60

Scanlon, Geraldine M., 131 n.3, 133 n.11
Scholes, Robert, 1

Shklovsky, Victor, 132 n.9
Shoemaker, William H., 69, 130–1 n.26, 133 n.1
Sinnigen, John, 131 n.22
Sobejano, Gonzalo, 89
Stern, Lawrence, *Tristram Shandy*, 100

Terry, Arthur, 77, 79, 132 n.15
Thackeray, William M., *Vanity Fair*, 98, 100
Tierno Galván, Enrique, 20, 21, 80, 133 n.23
Tolstoy, Leo, 1
Tomaschevsky, Boris, 102

Ullman, Stephen, 25, 34, 129–30 n.7, 130 n.20, 131 nn.1 and 2
Unamuno, Miguel de, *Niebla*, 70

Verdín Díaz, Guillermo, 24–5, 129–30 n.7, 130 nn.9, 20 and 22

White, Hayden, 79, 123–4, 126–7
Willis, Raymond, 67, 69, 132 n.4

Zeidner, Betty Jean, 131 n.4
Zola, Emile, 1, 27